THE NEW
BLOODY MARY

THE NEW
BLOODY MARY

More Than 75 Classics, Riffs &
Contemporary Recipes for the Modern Bar

VINCENZO MARIANELLA AND
JAMES O. FRAIOLI

CREATIVE CONSULTANT CHRISTINA KINDWALL
PHOTOGRAPHY BY JESSICA NICOSIA-NADLER
STYLING BY LE CORDON BLEU COLLEGE OF
CULINARY ARTS, SACRAMENTO, CALIFORNIA

Skyhorse Publishing

Skyhorse Publishing books may be purchased in bulk at special discounts for sales promotion, corporate gifts, fund-raising, or educational purposes. Special editions can also be created to specifications. For details, contact the Special Sales Department, Skyhorse Publishing, 307 West 36th Street, 11th Floor, New York, NY 10018 or info@skyhorsepublishing.com.

Skyhorse® and Skyhorse Publishing® are registered trademarks of Skyhorse Publishing, Inc.®, a Delaware corporation.

Visit our website at www.skyhorsepublishing.com.

10 9 8 7 6 5 4 3 2 1

Library of Congress Cataloging-in-Publication Data

Names: Marianella, Vincenzo, author. | Fraioli, James O. (Cookbook author), author.
Title: The New Bloody Mary: more than 75 classics, riffs & contemporary recipes for the modern bar / Vincenzo Marianella and James O. Fraioli; Creative Consultant Christina Kindwall; Photography by Jessica Nicosia Nadler; Styling by Le Cordon Bleu College of Culinary Arts, Sacramento, California.
Description: New York : Skyhorse Publishing, 2017. | Includes index.
Identifiers: LCCN 2016047555| ISBN 9781510716681 (hardback) | ISBN 9781510716698 (ebook)
Subjects: LCSH: Bloody Marys (Cocktails) | BISAC: COOKING / Beverages / Wine & Spirits. | COOKING / Beverages / Bartending. | COOKING / Specific Ingredients / Herbs, Spices, Condiments. | LCGFT: Cookbooks.
Classification: LCC TX951 .M2637 2017 | DDC 641.87/4—dc23
LC record available at https://lccn.loc.gov/2016047555

Cover design by Brian Peterson
Cover photo credit by Jessica Nicosia-Nadler

Printed in China

ACKNOWLEDGMENTS

The authors would like to greatly acknowledge the following people for their generous support and assistance with this book:

All of the contributing bartenders, mixologists, bloggers, bars, and restaurants. Without your unbelievable support and assistance, this book would not be possible;

Christina Kindwall for your countless hours of research, persistence, and dedication;

Photographer Jessica Nicosia Nadler;

The extraordinary culinary team at Le Cordon Bleu College of Culinary Arts, Sacramento, California: Chef John Hall M. Ed; Chef Vincent Paul; Alexander C.E.C., Chef Adrian Day; Murchison, Meghan Leeman, D. W. Herold, David Nadler, Gary Flora, Raymond Cordell;

The editorial team at Skyhorse Publishing;

Agent Sharlene Martin of Martin Literary & Media Management.

CONTENTS

INTRODUCTION

The old saying "as American as apple pie" is often used to illustrate something familiar and something comfortable. It could also be used to express a reflection of our societal ingenuity, independence, and our history—and let's face it, it also speaks to our gluttonous yet remedial nature. Perhaps the saying should actually be "as American as a Bloody Mary," since this iconic cocktail really is a blend of a little bit of our history, seasoned with a variety of regional and ethnic influences, shaken or stirred to create the most adaptable cocktail the world has ever known, yet it remains as American as apple pie.

Something about a Bloody Mary conjures up nostalgic feelings of relaxation, exploration, and remediation. The Bloody Mary is something truly remarkable. It is one of those cocktails that is time-tested yet so unique and special that many bartenders and mixologists feel they've been given a blank canvas in which to be creative, offering the consumer an alcoholic beverage that can be modified or specifically tailor-made to suit particular taste preferences. From an endless array of garnishes and condiments, to a variety of spirits including vodka, gin, beer, rum, and tequila, the Bloody Mary is as varied as the imagination allows. Virtually endless flavor profiles are created with each new combination. Then, of course, there are those who simply prefer the traditional Bloody Mary without any alteration. The choice is entirely up to the individual requesting the drink. As for the bartenders and mixologists crafting what many consider to be the most popular cocktail in America, it is also their nature to try and fully understand each beverage, its history, and ultimately, its intention. To fully understand the Bloody Mary cocktail, learn of its origin, and how it has evolved throughout the years, is really to understand a lot about who we are as a society.

The Bloody Mary is a little more than eighty years old, yet the tales and lore behind its origin are just as murky and mysterious as the libation itself. There are many colorful theories, some more disputed than others, for exactly who created the drink and when. We do know, however, that Paris, Prohibition, the Russian Revolution, Hollywood, and Hemingway are all key players in creating the Bloody Mary we know and admire today.

The year is 1911, and American jockey Ted Sloan appoints Scotsman Harry MacElhone to run a bar in Paris named Harry's New York Bar at 5 Rue Danou. Ted procured the site built around his favorite New York bar, which he had dismantled and sent by boat to Paris to create an authentic American bar as a way of preserving his favorite watering hole as Prohibition loomed in the States. An authentic New York-style bar became a novelty as liquor-deprived Americans, including servicemen and American celebrities such as Rita Hayworth, Ernest Hemingway, and Humphrey Bogart sought refuge at Harry's in Paris when Prohibition went into in full swing in the United States by 1920. As legend has it, the words *Sank Roo Doe Noo* were written on Harry's of Paris because that is what limited French-speaking Americans would tell the Parisian taxi drivers where to take them soon as they stepped off the plane.

At the same time, the Russian Revolution had dismantled the czarist autocracy and was leading to the rise of the Soviet Union, which sent émigrés fleeing Russia into France. Vladimir Smirnov, who took over his father's vodka company, was one of those who fled Russia, taking up residence in France, where he popularized vodka. Meanwhile, Ferdinand "Pete" Petiot experimented with vodka while bartending at Harry's bar.

Back in the United States, many brands were trying to capitalize on Prohibition by offering cocktail-deprived Americans with something to take their place. In the 1930s, Lea & Perrin's printed their recipe for Tomato Juice Cocktail, which was a combination of tomato juice mixed with Lea & Perrin's sauce and served ice-cold. It is believed at that time, back in France, that Petiot was introduced to this Tomato Juice Cocktail in a can and thought it could breathe life into his vodka, which he described as "a tasteless spirit." Yet, when he combined vodka with tomato juice and spices, something magical happened. That magic, many believe, resulted in the birth of the Bloody Mary.

There are also many theories for how the name *Bloody Mary* came to be. One of the most popular theories is that Petiot, who was born in England, named the drink after Queen Mary Tudor of England. Apparently, Queen Mary's "Bloody Mary" moniker came from her acts as queen in support of Catholicism, which killed hundreds of Protestants during the Marian Persecutions due to the Heresy Acts of 1554.

Another popular theory for how the name originated is that American entertainer Roy Barton often frequented

a dark and shady Chicago bar in the 1900s called the Bucket of Blood, named for all the blood mopped up from the floor after fights broke out. Barton also frequented jockey Ted Sloan's New York bar before it was dismantled and sent to Paris. There, he nicknamed a barmaid named Mary "Bloody Mary" since she once worked at the Bucket of Blood Bar in Chicago. It is said that this name was attached to the bar when it made its way to Paris, and therefore, attached to the drink. The name was then brought back to the States when Prohibition ended in 1933 and Vincent Astor brought over famed barman Petiot to man his impressively upscale King Cole Bar at the St. Regis Hotel in New York, New York, famous for its thirty-foot nursery rhyme mural by Maxfield Parrish. Unfortunately, the name Bloody Mary was deemed too vile for the upscale patrons of the St. Regis's King Cole Bar. To not offend the discerning clientele, Petiot was asked to rename his cocktail, which he did, calling it the Red Snapper. To this day, Petiot's Red Snapper is still served at the St. Regis Hotel King Cole Bar, consisting of vodka, tomato juice, Worcestershire sauce, Tabasco, salt, pepper, lemon juice, and a slim celery stick to stir the drink.

During World War II, and in the end of Prohibition, Vladimir Smirnov decided to sell the rights to Smirnov Vodka to the Heublin Company, famous for their A.1. Steak Sauce. Heublin began to market the "White Whiskey" in America while tying it in with the surging Bloody Mary movement. Like many products of the postwar period, the company hired a celebrity to advertise their product. One of the actors Smirnoff hired was famous comedian/singer/actor George Jessel, who promoted a new drink called the Tomato Pickup or Morning Glory, claiming the cocktail was a cure for his hangovers and could rejuvenate him prior to performances.

Regardless of who was first or who had more impact, thanks to the combination of Petiot's influence in popularizing the Red Snapper to the many celebrities, socialites, and New York elite at the St. Regis Hotel, and George Jessel's many celebrity endorsements for the salty and savory vodka cocktail in mainstream advertising and culture, the Bloody Mary now seemed *en vogue* in prestigious circles, continuing to capture the attention of cocktail consumers worldwide.

Further evidence that the Bloody Mary had, in fact, made its way onto the global stage was through author Ernest Hemingway, who notably consumed many Bloody Marys during his visits to Harry's New York Bar in Paris during the 1920s. He wrote in a letter in 1947 that he had introduced the Bloody Mary to Hong Kong in 1941, which, he said, "Did more than any other single factor except the Japanese Army to precipitate the fall of that Crown Colony." Hemingway had very specific instructions on how to make the cocktail:

"To make a pitcher of Blood Marys (any smaller amount is worthless) take a good sized pitcher and put in it as big a lump of ice as it will hold. (This to prevent too rapid melting and watering of the product.) Mix a pint of good Russian vodka and an equal amount of chilled tomato juice. Add a tablespoon full of Worchester Sauce. Lea & Perrins is usual, but can use A1 or any good beefsteak sauce. Stir, and then add a jigger of fresh squeezed lime juice. Stir. Then add small amounts of celery salt, cayenne pepper, and black pepper. Keep on stirring and taste to see how it is doing. If you get it too powerful weaken with more tomato juice. If it lacks authority add more vodka."

Despite the many murky theories for the origin of the drink itself, one point is clear: the Bloody Mary is tied to many historically significant periods in history, which it still embraces today, but it has now evolved to embrace the ingenuity and creativity of those who created it, and is so adaptable that it can be adopted by any culture as their own. This is what makes the Bloody Mary so iconic, classic, and timeless—and why it's important to never forget the original recipes that started it all while still appreciating how the drink has metamorphosed over time, leading us to today's Bloody Mary, which remains as American as apple pie.

Throughout the pages of this book, bartenders, mixologists, bloggers, and representatives of bars and restaurants, including co-author Vincenzo Marianella himself, have proudly offered their personal recipes for the Bloody Mary during the authors' ultimate quest to collect some of the best classic and contemporary recipes for the famous cocktail and share them with others under one cover. The recipes ahead truly represent just how far the Bloody Mary has come, and how far it will continue to go, while still remaining true to its heritage. This book is dedicated to honoring the Bloody Mary, and the many ways to prepare it, so that we never lose sight of such an iconic cocktail. Let's raise a glass and toast to the importance of preserving the Bloody Mary, including all its glorious forms.

TOOLS OF THE TRADE

Whether you're a professional mixologist or a backyard bartender, having the right tools and equipment is essential. And just like a true craftsman, the tools and equipment you use should be well made and feel good in the hand. Obviously, you will find a lot of tools, equipment, and gadgets out there, and it's difficult to mention every one, but listed are the items you should have on hand to get you started. Most can be found at your local kitchen store or at online retailers like Amazon.com.

Bar Spoon

A long solid metal bar spoon with a twist down the middle of the base means you got your hands on the right spoon. Get one that feels good in your hand.

Blenders

A quality countertop blender is necessary when blending ice and small or chopped ingredients. Always make sure the lid is secure before turning on the machine. This may sound like an obvious step, but you'll be unpleasantly surprised if that lid is loose. For finer ingredients like liquids and herbs, an immersion blender will do the trick.

If you have money to spend, the ideal blender is a commercial drink blender, like Vitamix. They're well worth the money if you frequently make cocktails that call for a variety of fruits and vegetables to be blended, like the Nola Verde Bloody Mary (page 114).

Bottles and Containers

For the various spirit-infusions and Bloody Mary mixes featured in this book, you'll need bottles and containers in which to store the liquids. Most infusions and mixes can be stored in glass bottles like empty liquor bottles. You can also add a pour spout to the bottle for easy pouring like the pros. Sealed glass jars like Mason jars are also good for storing liquids. The more decorative the vessels, the nicer they will look on your counter or shelf.

Cutting Board

Wood is good, but plastic works, too. You'll want different sizes—large for cutting up ingredients like pineapples and watermelons, and small to keep beside the bar to slice up lemons, limes, and other small fruit, vegetables, and herbs. If you decide to go with plastic, try to find a black board instead of white. Black hides the stains.

Ice Bucket and Tongs

An insulated bucket with a lid is always good to have, especially when needing to preserve your ice on hot summer days. Speaking of ice . . .

Most Bloody Marys in this book call for ice, so you'll need plenty of ice on hand. The best ice for cocktails is clear ice. The bags of ice at your local supermarket are clear ice, and the larger the cubes, the better (unless you're blending). Home freezer ice is fine and convenient, but is typically cloudy in appearance and can take on an aftertaste because of the recycled air in your refrigerator-freezer. Ideally, a home ice machine that produces clear ice is the way to go, but a bag of ice from the market is perfect for the job.

Jigger

A two-sided jigger is for measuring your alcohol pours, and they come in different sizes. Invest in a quality metal jigger, especially those that delineate a variety of fractions.

Juicer

Like the blender, a quality juicer is the perfect kitchen companion when making many of the Bloody Mary mixes in this book. Invest in a good electric model, especially if you're going to juice a lot of fruit and vegetables. If you're old-fashioned, a handheld juicer works well, but requires more elbow grease. In a pinch, you can also use a reamer.

Kitchen-Bar Rags

Make sure the rags can absorb liquids, as their function is to clean up spills. Damp rags seem to work better than dry.

Knife

Always use a high-quality knife and always keep it sharp. Typically, you'll want a small knife for slicing small fruits and vegetables, and a larger one for cutting items like pineapples and watermelon.

Microplane

This fine grater is ideal for adding zest to a cocktail or as a garnish on top. Microplane seems to be the authority on graters.

Muddler

This handheld rod with a rounded bottom is used to extract herbal essences and crush fruits and other ingredients in the bottom of the glass. Wood muddlers are ideal, but plastic will work fine, too.

Peeler

The Y-shaped peeler gives you more control and cleaner garnishes, like the twist, but in a pinch, you can always use that vegetable peeler in your kitchen drawer.

Shaker

A quality cobbler shaker is preferred, which consists of three interlocking stainless steel pieces: the cup, the strainer, and the cap. The built-in strainer means one less tool to grab to finish the Bloody Mary. You can also use a mixing glass and a Hawthorne strainer, but this is generally for stirring—not shaking—cocktails.

Spice Grinder

These small grinders are perfect when working with fresh spices. Just look at the Danish Mary (page 87) and you'll understand why. The blade in this compact-sized grinder is designed specifically to grind spices and nuts with a touch of a button. This item can be found in any quality kitchen store or online.

Stainless Steel Cream Whipper

This tool isn't a necessity, but is particularly handy if you like to make drinks with creams and foams on top, like the 7452 Mary (page 57). This tool can also be found in any quality kitchen store or online.

Strainers

If you're making Bloody Marys with a shaker that doesn't have a built-in strainer, like the cobbler shaker, make sure you have a Hawthorne strainer. This tool has a curved metal coil that allows you to adjust the level of the strain. A julep strainer, which is bowl-shaped and slotted with small holes, also allows you to strain liquid. Whatever strainer you prefer, make sure it's good quality. The strainer should feel heavy, not flimsy, and, if going for the Hawthorne model, have a nice tight and sturdy coil.

GLASSWARE & SERVING VESSELS

Most of the Bloody Mary recipes showcased in this book are served in either pint glasses or Mason jars, with a few finding their way into a coupe or wine glass. Because this new collection of recipes includes twists and riffs on the iconic beverage, feel free to experiment with different vessels to present your handcrafted Bloody Mary, like those illustrated in many of the photographs. As the old adage goes, "variety is the spice of life," so remember, the glass, cup, or bowl you choose represents the foundation of the drink. Thinking outside of the box will help make your cocktails look more hip and stylish at your next gathering. Also, any vessel that will not be getting ice should be kept chilled before serving. Here are some recommended vessels in which to serve your next Bloody Mary:

Collins Glass

A tall, cylindrical glass with plenty of room for ice that holds between 8 and 14 ounces.

Coupe

Supposedly molded from Marie Antoinette's left breast, this rounded yet elegant old-fashioned champagne glass is now used for modern cocktails and holds around 5 to 7 ounces.

Flute

With a tall, narrow bowl on a stem, typically reserved for champagne, this glass holds between 4 and 6 ounces.

Highball

Named for a railroad instrument that indicated speed, this is a cross between a Collins glass and a rocks glass that hold from 8 to 12 ounces.

Hurricane Glass

Resembling a glass-footed hurricane lantern, this vessel can hold 12 to 20 ounces.

Martini Glass

An enlarged, modified coupe with a V-shape, this can hold anywhere from 8 to 16 ounces.

Mason Jar

A glass jar used for canning that has glass screw threads around the neck to accommodate a metal lid. This vessel can also hold 8 to 16 ounces.

Pilsner Glass

A Collins glass with attitude that tapers inward toward the bottom and holds between 8 and 12 ounces.

Pint Glass

A 16-ounce glass either in an inverted conical shape or with a swelling at the top.

Rocks Glass

A short, cylindrical glass used for drinks that either get no ice or a few cubes. It can hold between 6 and 8 ounces. Large glasses can hold 10 to 12 ounces.

Snifter

A short, round bowl that has a narrow mouth and a glass foot that can hold around 6 to 8 ounces. Good when serving cocktails with crushed ice.

Wine Glass

Comes in a variety of sizes and shapes, with a large opening and a narrow stem attached to a glass foot.

TECHNIQUES

Now that you have the tools you need, and the vessels in which to serve your Bloody Marys, it's time to quickly go over the common techniques that will enable you to make the vast majority of drinks featured in this book.

Blending

You'll discover that a fair share of blending is involved when making the various Bloody Mary mixes in this book. For simple mixes with small ingredients, use an immersion blender if you have one. (Just make sure the blades are well below the liquid or you'll be wearing your Bloody Mary.) For countertop blenders when mixing larger ingredients, pulse in short bursts. This will help break up what you put inside without breaking the motor.

Chilling

This pertains to the vessels prior to serving. Try to keep an assortment of glasses in the freezer, especially on hot summer days. This makes the Bloody Mary that much colder and more

refreshing. If you don't have room in your freezer, fill the glasses with ice and a little cold water while you're making the drink. By the time you've collected the ingredients and taken care of the necessary prep work, you should have chilled glasses ready for your cocktail.

Straining

Unless you are building a drink in the glass it will be served in, which some of the recipes call for, you will likely strain the freshly made cocktail into a new vessel. As previously mentioned, the Cobbler shaker has a built-in strainer and will do the work for you after you shake the drink and are ready to pour. If you are stirring or using another type of shaker, you will need to grab a Hawthorne strainer to separate the ice from your handcrafted Bloody Mary.

Rimming

Many of the Bloody Marys in this book including rimming the glass with various salts and seasonings. To do so, begin by running the garnish (lime wedge, lemon

wedge, jalapeño, fruit or vegetable slice, etc.) around the edge of the glass to moisten the rim, making sure the outside edge is well covered. Then slowly roll the moistened outer rim in the prepared salt or seasonings that have been spread out in a thin layer on a plate or paper towel for easy clean up. The flavored rim is to add another layer of taste without incorporating it into the drink, which would alter its flavor profile.

Stirring

Some of the Bloody Mary recipes call for stirring, not shaking. This means you are not adding air into the cocktail, but simply chilling and diluting the drink. This is where the bar spoon comes in. Try to stir in a clear glass. This will allow you to look for the visual clues that signal when the drink is ready. For instance, you should be left with an ice-cold beverage devoid of any imperfections like ice shards or cloudiness from aeration.

Shaking

Shaking, which is the opposite of stirring, is performed when you vigorously aerate the mixture to "wake it up." This is often done using a Cobbler shaker, and it's not a vertical up and down motion. Do it like the pros by shaking horizontally using two hands typically over one shoulder. A good shake should last 15 to 20 seconds before you strain. Just make sure the cap's on tight—you want to shake the drink, not shower the person who happens to be standing behind you.

Muddling

When muddling herbs and other botanicals, press firmly to extract the essences and oils, but don't smash the herbs. Press harder to crush small fruits.

A NOTE ON STORAGE AND SHELF LIFE

Because the majority of the Bloody Mary recipes come from various bars and restaurants, the house-made infusions and mixes featured in this book are used in a timely fashion due to customer demand. It's not often that a popular infusion or mix will sit for longer than one week. Home bartenders should be aware that the recipes offered are not intended for long shelf life. Some recipes may indicate how long it can last on the shelf or in the refrigerator, others may not. A general rule of thumb is that any infusion or mix with perishable ingredients and/or stored in the refrigerator should last several days, sometimes up to one week. For the spirit-infusions that consist of just alcohol and dry ingredients, you can pretty much anticipate an indefinite shelf life.

TODAY'S BLOODY MARY BAR

Have you ever walked into a party, bar, or restaurant and feasted your eyes on a custom Bloody Mary bar? Oh, it is a beautiful sight to behold. As though we are children exploring a candy store, the variety of colors and cornucopia of yummy eats immediately draws our attention. It makes us eager to display our creativity and enjoyment of favorite tastes by selecting what goes in our glass from the delicious bounty displayed on a beautifully decorated table. Best of all, a Bloody Mary bar can be easily duplicated at home.

To begin, you'll need a sturdy table with plenty of room. A tablecloth is always a nice touch. Try to select a variety of different sized and colored bowls and serving trays to hold the condiments. Large retailers and discounted shops are ideal places to find a variety of decorative bowls and vessels. Vintage and second-hand stores, even garage sales, are good places to find vintage serving sets to give your Bloody Mary bar a distinguished look.

You will also want to have a chilled appetizer-serving tray on hand to display and keep your perishable foods fresh. Have fun with labels describing the various condiments by using a chalkboard or artistically printed or handmade signs to describe all the drink options.

Here are some general steps to get you going:

Step 1: Like a food buffet line, begin at one side of the table, placing all of your clean drinking vessels (no fingerprints please) on a fancy serving tray. Next to the tray, arrange several pitchers of some of the different color (yellow, orange, green, red) Bloody Mary mixes featured in this book. You'll want the mixes cold, so display them in a shallow, stylish party tub filled with crushed ice.

Step 2: Create a salt and seasoning rim station by placing several large saucers in a triangle with each saucer containing different salt and seasoning rims, which are also featured throughout

this book. (A few extra bonus recipes at the end of this chapter offer additional options.) Next to the saucers, include a bowl full of citrus wedges (limes, lemons, and oranges) to moisten the rims. Make sure to label each rim salt and seasoning, and include what rims pair best with the other ingredients on the table.

Step 3: On a serving tray next to the pitchers of colorful mixes, arrange the liquor options and the ice bucket and tongs. As you'll find throughout this book, the list of liquor selections and infusions are long and varied. Select a few to display, as it's always nice to see bottles of tequila, bourbon, gin, and an interesting infusion next to that plain ol' bottle of vodka.

Step 4: Next, place the condiments and garnishes in a variety of serving bowls or trays, and arrange on a large serving tray. Make sure all perishable items like seafood, cheese, and vegetables are served on ice, and include a stylish container filled with cocktail picks and skewers. Don't forget plenty of cocktail napkins and a couple bar spoons for stirring (for a Bloody Mary bar, it's best to have guests stir their drinks and not shake, so leave the shaker off the table and thereby avoid unnecessary spills and cleanups).

As mentioned, throughout this book you'll find plenty of recipes and examples of what to display at your next Bloody Mary bar, along with some bonus recipes and suggestions below.

The New Bloody Mary Bar

an assortment of different shaped
  cocktail glasses (page 11)
3 or 4 glass pitchers to hold the
  colorful Bloody Mary mixes
tub with ice
3 or 4 saucers for the rim station with
  citrus wedges
large ice bucket with claw tongs
8 or 10 bowls, serving dishes, and trays
  (different colors and shapes) for
  condiments
cocktail napkins, picks, and 6-inch
  bamboo skewers
bar spoons

Spirits
  1 bottle premium vodka
  1 bottle of vodka-infusion
  1 bottle premium dry gin
  1 bottle mezcal

Bloody Mary Mixes
  yellow Bloody Mary mix
  orange Bloody Mary mix
  classic Bloody Mary mix
  green/verde Bloody Mary mix

Condiments and Garnishes

 Tabasco hot sauce
 Crystal Louisiana hot sauce
 Sriracha hot chili sauce
 clam juice
 Worcestershire sauce
 pepperoncinis
 pickle spears
 hearts of palm
 pickled Brussels sprouts
 pickled beets
 taqueria-style pickled carrots and
  jalapeños*
 blue-cheese stuffed olives
 cheese cubes (Dubliner or Colby
  Jack)
 cured salami cubes
 jumbo prawns
 pickled herring
 lemon wheels
 lime wheels
 thinly sliced celery spears
 cherry tomatoes (yellow and red)
 Bacon-Wrapped Cherry Peppers,
  recipe follows

BACON-WRAPPED CHERRY PEPPERS:

6 hot cherry peppers, halved through
 the stem, seeded, drained, and
 patted dry
1 (8-oz) package soft cream cheese
12 extra-thin bacon slices

Preheat the oven to 350°F.

 Stuff each cherry pepper half with a heaping teaspoon of cream cheese and wrap with a slice of bacon. Secure with a toothpick.

 Arrange the stuffed peppers in a large ovenproof skillet and cook over moderate heat, turning, until the bacon is browned, about 12 to 15 minutes. Transfer the skillet to the oven, and bake for about 5 minutes, or until the bacon is crisp and the cream cheese is hot. Serve the stuffed cherry peppers when still warm.

---

*Available at most Hispanic grocery stores or the Hispanic aisle at supermarket

LEMON-INFUSED VODKA

Not only does this home-infused vodka smell like fresh-cut lemons, but it also takes on a perfect shade of soft yellow.

Makes about 2 cups
---

3 medium lemons, rinsed and
    quartered
2 cups premium vodka
1 quart Mason jar with lid (or any jar
    with a sealing lid)

Place the lemons and vodka in the Mason jar and seal. Place in a dark, cool place and test for flavor after one week. Continue to infuse for 2 to 3 weeks, or until vodka has taken on the desired depth of flavor. Discard the lemons and strain the vodka into a clean, clear, sealable bottle. Store until needed.

SOUTHWEST SALT RIM

2 tablespoons Lawry's Seasoned Salt
2 tablespoons Tajin Clásico
1 teaspoon Smoked Chipotle Chili
    Pepper

SCANDINAVIAN SALT RIM

2 tablespoons sea salt (or coarse kosher
    salt)
1 teaspoon dried dill weed
1 teaspoon celery seed

OLD SCHOOL SALT RIM

2 tablespoons Old Bay Seasoning
1 teaspoon fresh cracked, coarse-
    ground black pepper
1 teaspoon celery salt

In this chapter . . .

CLASSIC SNAPPERS, BULLS & MARIAS

When you're in the mood for something original, or a cocktail with history, try one of the Bloody Mary recipes in the pages ahead . . . with a few added surprises.

The Red Snapper is the original Bloody Mary, made first with vodka then later gin, the spirit representative in Snappers today. Add some beef bouillon or beef broth to the Bloody Mary and you have yourself an old-school Bull Shot. This popular beef broth cocktail originated in the late 1950s and appeared in most steakhouses across America. It was also the drink of choice among celebrities in the sixties and seventies, including Richard Chamberlain and Joan Crawford. In Canada, around the same time, bartenders were adding Clamato (a blend of tomato juice and clam broth) to their Bloody Marys, calling it the Bloody Caesar. And those who opted to replace the traditional vodka with tequila or mezcal found themselves drinking a Bloody Maria. Today, all these iconic cocktails—both in their original form and with a twist—can still be found, admired, and appreciated if you just know where to look.

RED SNAPPER
—— (THE ORIGINAL BLOODY MARY) ——

The legend of the Bloody Mary is still often disputed. The classic drink began as tomato juice and vodka, but in 1934, French bartender Fernand Petiot at Harry's Bar in Paris perfected the cocktail by combining the original tomato and vodka formula, then added lemon juice, a couple dashes of celery salt, black pepper, and cayenne pepper, and some Worcestershire sauce. When Fernand left Paris for New York's St. Regis Hotel, he swapped the vodka for gin and named his creation the Red Snapper (because Bloody Mary was deemed inappropriate for the hotel's elegant clientele). Today, Bartender Bill Dante at King Cole Bar & Salon at the St. Regis still serves Petiot's 1934 classic. Considered one of the most popular drinks at the hotel, Dante insists you must stick to the original recipe (with vodka) and follow Petiot's exact instructions when making the Red Snapper. If it's not in the original drink, Dante won't add it.

Serves 1

1 ounce premium vodka (or gin)
2 ounces tomato juice
1 dash lemon juice
2 dashes celery salt
2 dashes fresh ground black pepper
2 dashes cayenne pepper
3 dashes Worcestershire sauce
lemon wedge, for garnish

Fill a glass with ice, and add the vodka.

In a cocktail shaker filled with ice, add the tomato juice, lemon juice, celery salt, black pepper, cayenne pepper, and the Worcestershire sauce. Shake vigorously, and strain over the prepared glass. Garnish and serve.

LATIN SNAPPER

Sebastian Hamilton-Mudge, an International Brand Ambassador for Beefeater Gin, created the Latin Snapper after numerous trips to Latin America where he taught gin and cocktail master classes. He also discovered during his educational tenure that the quality standard of bars and restaurants he visited in Buenos Aires, Mexico City, and across Colombia is fantastic and inspired him to write a number of recipes. Unlike the Red Snapper (previous page) and similar versions, which some may find to be thick and heavy, the Latin Snapper is light, fresh, and citrusy and often complements the warm climate, flavors, and atmosphere of the region. The coupette glass also gives this beverage a sexy and sophisticated touch.

Serves 1

1 ripe heirloom tomato (gold and green) or 4–5 heirloom cherry tomatoes
2 large sprigs fresh cilantro
1 small pinch sea salt
1 small pinch fresh ground black pepper
1½ ounces Beefeater Dry Gin
¾ ounce fresh lime juice
½ ounce simple syrup
2 or 3 dashes Tabasco Hot Sauce (or more depending on your taste)
sprig of fresh cilantro, for garnish

Chop the tomatoes and add to a cocktail shaker with the cilantro, sea salt, and black pepper. Muddle until well combined. Then add the gin, lime juice, simple syrup, hot sauce, and ice. Shake vigorously and strain into a chilled coupette glass. Garnish and serve.

MONTFORD SNAPPER

When Sebastian Hamilton-Mudge, the International Brand Ambassador for Beefeater Gin featured in the previous recipe, prepared for a group of high-profile American journalists arriving to the London distillery, he made sure a selection of Red Snappers would be waiting for them—all made with gin, of course. This became the catalyst for Sebastian and Tim Stones, his colleague, along with other global ambassadors for Beefeater Gin, to craft yet another new recipe. Refreshing, healthy, and beautiful in color, the Montford Snapper, named after Montford Place, the address of the distillery, offers dynamic character and flavor nuances that complement its sweet and savory nature.

Serves 1

1½ ounces Beefeater Dry Gin
Montford Snapper Mix, as needed, recipe follows
sprig of fresh Italian (flat-leaf) parsley and a lemon slice, for garnish

In a highball glass, add some cubed or hand-chipped ice. Pour in the gin (feel free to add more based on your preference). Pour the Montford Snapper Mix over the gin to the top of the glass and give it a stir to mix. Garnish and serve.

MONTFORD SNAPPER MIX

1½ ounces good-quality tomato juice
1 ounce fresh beetroot juice
1 ounce fresh blood orange juice
½ ounce fresh carrot juice
¼ ounce fresh lemon juice

¼ ounce simple syrup
1 small pinch sea salt
1 small pinch fresh ground black pepper
2 dashes Tabasco Hot Sauce, or to taste

In a suitable container, add the tomato, beetroot, blood orange, carrot, and lemon juices. Stir in the simple syrup, sea salt, black pepper, and hot sauce. Mix well to combine, and refrigerate for at least 3 hours.

BULL SHOT

The Bull Moose Room at New York City's Keens Steakhouse features an array of memorabilia, including a massive bull moose head in honor of President Theodore Roosevelt, who used to frequent the restaurant. Since 1885, enormous steaks and famed mutton chops have been enjoyed at this iconic eatery, along with classic cocktails from within the Bloody Mary family. According to Bonnie Jenkins at Keens, the Bull Shot is one such drink their well-seasoned diners find synonymous with this old-school steakhouse and often request.

Serves 1

2 ounces premium vodka
2 ounces beef bouillon
½ ounce fresh lemon juice
1 large pinch fresh ground black pepper
2 dashes Worcestershire sauce

Fill a glass with ice.

In a shaker filled with ice, add the vodka, beef bouillon, lemon juice, black pepper, and Worcestershire sauce. Shake well to combine, and pour into the prepared glass.

BELLE AND BULL

When blogger Darby Doyle, a.k.a. the Bourbon Gal in Utah, went skiing last season and ran out of vodka during her slope-side tailgate, she reached for a flask of whiskey stashed inside her parka and the Belle and Bull was born. This burly Bloody brings a bit of umami to the flavor profile of the traditional bevy with the addition of hearty beef stock and bold bourbon. It makes for a satisfying stick-to-your-ribs version of the classic, especially with an addition of steak seasoning to the rim and a beef jerky garnish. When making this recipe, go for a spicy rye-forward bourbon such as Woodford Reserve or Belle Meade to add a bit of kick and balance to this savory medley. Although most citrus cocktails work best in a shaker, take the time to stir this one thoroughly. If you don't, you'll end up with a pale pink frothy mess—definitely not the vibe we're going for in this bourbon twist.

Serves 1

Rim
lemon wedge
1 tablespoon steak seasoning mix

2 ounces bourbon whiskey (Woodford Reserve or Belle Meade)
1½ ounces Wild Game Stock, recipe on page 31 (or use store-bought organic beef stock)

1 generous pinch steak seasoning mix (McCormick Grill Mates Smokehouse Maple)
⅛ teaspoon prepared horseradish
½ lemon, juiced
1 generous pinch fresh coarse-ground black pepper
5–6 ounces pulp-free tomato juice
smoky beef jerky, for garnish

Rim a heavy pint glass (page 13) with the steak seasoning mix, and add 4 or 5 ice cubes.

In a mixing glass filled with ice, add the bourbon whiskey, Wild Game Stock, steak seasoning mix, prepared horseradish, lemon juice, black pepper, and tomato juice. Stir thoroughly with a long-handled bar spoon until combined, and pour into the prepared glass. Add more ice if needed to fill the glass. Garnish and serve.

---

*The molasses and brown sugar elements of McCormick Grill Mates Smokehouse Maple makes for a nice sweet note under the bourbon's spice.

—— WILD GAME STOCK ——

This is an ideal recipe if you have a bunch of beef and venison bones on hand. Otherwise, your local butcher should be able to provide you with what you need. Ask for bones with some meat attached. Bones from leftover roasts and steaks also work well. Simply fill freezer bags with the bones and store in the freezer. The stock freezes well, too. You can even pour into ice cube trays, freeze, and pop them into freezer bags until you're ready to flavor gravy, sauces, and drinks, like the Belle and Bull.

Makes about 3 quarts

4 pounds beef and/or venison bones
2 tablespoons kosher salt
1 tablespoon fresh coarse-ground black pepper
1 onion, peeled and quartered
2 carrots, peeled and cut into 2-inch pieces
2 ribs celery, cut into 2-inch pieces

1 large clove garlic, peeled and smashed
2–3 tablespoons canola oil
1 sprig fresh rosemary
1 sprig fresh thyme
1 bay leaf
1 gallon (16 cups) cold water

Preheat oven to 425°F.

In a large mixing bowl, add the bones, kosher salt, black pepper, onion, carrots, celery, and garlic. Add the canola oil, making sure the bones are well coated. Arrange the bones and vegetables in an even layer on a rimmed baking sheet. Place in oven on center rack, and roast for 20 minutes. Turn bones over to cook evenly. Continue roasting for another 20 to 30 minutes, or until most of the vegetables have broken down and dark, crispy brown bits cover the bones. Remove from oven.

Add the roasted bones and vegetables to a large stock pot and scrape in all of the crispy bits stuck to the baking sheet along with remaining juices. Add the rosemary, thyme, bay leaf, and cold water. Cover and bring to a boil, then reduce to a simmer, allowing some steam to escape from the lid. Simmer on very low heat for 8 to 9 hours, making sure the liquid isn't boiling. Occasionally skim the foam collecting on the top and discard. The stock should be a dark mahogany brown and reduced by about one-third. Strain the stock and bones through a colander to remove any large pieces from stock. Let cool to room temperature. Skim off any fat or oil on the surface of the stock. Strain again through a double layer of cheesecloth to remove as many particles as possible (this will help keep the stock clear). Refrigerate for up to 1 week or freeze for up to 6 months.

— BROOKLYN BLOODY BULL—

The inspiration for this cocktail comes from a steakhouse drink called the Bull Shot. New York's Keens Steakhouse makes a great one (page 29), a combination of beef stock and Worcestershire sauce. In this version from Simon Gibson of New York's Brooklyn Star, the beef stock adds texture and depth while maintaining a thickness throughout the drink. The secret to Simon's cocktail is Guinness beer. The Irish stout shows up both in the homemade beef broth and in the drink itself. The beer ups the cocktail's umami quotient and gives the drink body and a touch of froth.

Serves 1

2 ounces premium vodka (Titos)
1 ounce Beef Stock, recipe on page 33
5 ounces Bloody Mary Mix,
recipe on page 33
1 splash Guinness Stout beer
pickled spicy string beans and cracked pepper, for garnish

In a pint glass filled with ice, add the vodka, Beef Stock, Bloody Mary Mix, and beer. Use the rock and roll method to mix: using two glasses, simply pour back and forth to give it a good mix. Never shake a Bloody Bull; it will dilute the drink too much. Garnish and serve.

BEEF STOCK

Makes about 1 gallon

6 beef shanks, roasted on grill or under
    broiler until browned
1½ cups Guinness beer
2 roasted tomatoes, prepared on grill or
    under broiler, chopped
3 roasted garlic cloves, prepared on grill
    or under broiler, peeled
1 charred onion, prepared on grill or
    under broiler, peeled and chopped
4 sprigs fresh thyme
2 bay leaves
¾ ounce fresh ground black pepper
cold water to cover 2 gallons

In a large stockpot over medium heat,
add the beef shanks, beer, roasted
tomatoes, garlic cloves, charred onion,
thyme, bay leaves, and black pepper.
Add the cold water. Bring to a boil,
then reduce heat to low and simmer
until the liquid is reduced by half.
Remove from heat, and strain into a
suitable container. Let cool. Store in
refrigerator until ready to use.

BLOODY MARY MIX

Makes about ¾ gallon

6 ounces dill pickle juice
1½ ounces kosher salt
1 ounce fresh cracked black pepper
2 ounces Worcestershire sauce
2½ ounces prepared horseradish
½ ounce Sambal Pepper Sauce
1 ounce Frank's Redhot Sauce
2¾ quarts tomato juice
1¼ cups fresh lemon juice

In a large, sealable container, combine
the pickle juice, kosher salt, black
pepper, Worcestershire sauce, prepared
horseradish, pepper sauce, hot sauce,
tomato juice, and lemon juice. Mix
well, and place the container in the
refrigerator until ready to use.

NOTE

The Mix, which can be kept refrigerated for up to 1 week, is much better
when prepared 1 or 2 days in advance, allowing the spices and flavors to
combine and balance.

——— BLOODY CAESAR ———

As legend has it, bartender Walter Chell at the Calgary Inn in Alberta (renamed the Calgary Westin Hotel), invented the infamous Bloody Caesar cocktail in 1969. He had been asked to concoct a drink to commemorate the opening of Marco's, the hotel's new Italian restaurant. Using the Italian dish Spaghetti alle vongole *for inspiration, Walter came up with a mixture of hand-mashed clams, tomato juice, vodka, Worcestershire sauce, salt, and pepper, which he named the Bloody Caesar after the Roman Emperor. Later, after consulting with Walter, the Mott Company went on to develop Clamato juice, made with a proprietary blend of tomato juice, spices, and clam broth. Today, more than 350 million Bloody Caesars are consumed every year in Canada, particularly at the Keg Steakhouse housed inside the Calgary Westin Hotel, the birthplace of the iconic beverage.*

Serves 1

Rim
celery salt

1½ ounces premium vodka
6 ounces Clamato juice (or make your own, page 39)
1 dash Worcestershire sauce
1 dash Tabasco Hot Sauce
1 pinch salt
1 pinch fresh ground black pepper
lime or lemon wheels, for garnish

Rim a glass with celery salt (page 13). In a separate glass, add the vodka, then fill the glass with some ice. Add the Clamato juice, Worcestershire sauce, hot sauce, salt, and black pepper. Use the rock and roll method to mix: using two glasses, simply pour back and forth to give it a good mix. Pour the contents into the prepared glass. Garnish and serve.

— JIMMY'S BLOODY BULL —

For those who are not big fans of vodka because of its lack of flavor, try substituting mezcal in your next bloody. That's what Jimmy Yeager of Jimmy's in Aspen, Colorado, did, and now his Bloody Bull is a hit with the après-ski crowd coming in to celebrate another epic day on the slopes of the Colorado Rockies. Jimmy adds a beefy and smoky mezcal to the cocktail, which blends perfectly with the earthiness of the tomato. His choice is Santo Domingo Albarradas from Del Maguey Mezcal. This bold and extremely smooth mezcal hails from Palenques, the beautiful distillery region in the remote mountains of the Sierra Madre south of Oaxaca, Mexico.

Serves 1

Rim
kosher salt
Tajin Clásico Seasoning

2 ounces premium mezcal (Santo Domingo Albarradas Del Maguey Single Village Mezcal)
¾ ounce fresh lime juice
6 ounces Jimmy's Bloody Mary Mix
Guinness Stout floater
lime or lemon wheel, for garnish

Rim a chilled Collins glass (page 13) with a blend of the kosher salt and Tajin, then fill with ice. Add the mezcal followed by the lime juice and Bloody Mary Mix. Stir well, and top with Guinness Stout. Garnish and serve.

JIMMY'S BLOODY MARY MIX

Makes about 1 quart

1 quart tomato juice
6 ounces fresh lime juice
1 ounce Tapatío Hot Sauce
1 ounce Worcestershire sauce
1 teaspoon fresh horseradish, ground
1 teaspoon Dijon mustard
1 teaspoon celery salt
1 teaspoon kosher salt
1 teaspoon fresh ground black pepper

In a suitable container, add the tomato juice, lime juice, hot sauce, Worcestershire sauce, horseradish, Dijon mustard, celery salt, kosher salt, and black pepper. Mix well and refrigerate until ready to use.

BLOODY MARIA

This cocktail is a classic twist on the Bloody Mary, but with a bit of Latin flair. Jen Ackrill of Rye in San Francisco, California, shares her secret Bloody Maria recipe, which she calls the spicy Latina sister of the Bloody Mary. The tasteful garnish she serves it with is popular with her patrons, who prefer a light snack, but don't want to get bogged down with food.

Serves 1

2 ounces premium tequila (Silver or Anejo)
4 ounces tomato juice
½ ounce fresh lemon juice
4 dashes Worcestershire sauce
2 dashes Tabasco Hot Sauce
2 dashes Tapatío Hot sauce
1 tablespoon horseradish, finely grated
1 pinch celery salt
1 dash fresh ground black pepper
lime wedge, lemon wedge, cucumber spear, cocktail spear with a combination of sweet peppers, jalapeño and Mexican Queso Fresco, for garnish

Fill a pint glass with ice.

In a shaker filled with ice, add the tequila, tomato juice, lemon juice, Worcestershire sauce, hot sauces, horseradish, celery salt, and black pepper. Give it 1 to 3 light shakes, avoiding dilution. Strain into the prepared glass. Garnish and serve.

CAESAR'S GHOST

In Canada, the go-to brunch drink is the Bloody Caesar (previous page). Almost identical to America's traditional Bloody Mary, the main differences are Clamato instead of tomato juice and lime garnish instead of lemon. At Seattle's famous cocktail bar Canon, now ranked one of the top bars in the world, co-owner and bar manager Jamie Boudreau ups the game by making a Clamato Mix from scratch (recipe below). Appearances matter, so for this drink, Jamie clarifies the liquid to make it see-through, almost ghostly. Despite the extra work, or maybe because of it, this is truly a delicious beverage, packed with flavor and much lighter in body than the heavier, thicker Bloody Mary. The Akvavit (also spelled Aquavit) is an old Scandinavian herbal liqueur with notes of caraway and dill.

Serves 1

Rim
lime wedge
celery salt

1½ ounces gin
½ ounce Akvavit Scandinavian liqueur
4 ounces Clamato Mix, recipe on page 39
pickled asparagus, cherry tomato, lime wedge, for garnish

Rim a Collins glass (page 13) with celery salt, and fill the glass with ice. Add the gin and Akvavit. Top with the Clamato Mix. Garnish and serve.

CANON'S CLAMATO MIX

Makes about 3 liters

3 cups distilled water
4 ounces organic vegetable stock
1 ounce dashi Japanese soup base powder
20 ounces canned roasted tomatoes
18 ounces canned diced tomatoes
3 ounces canned tomato paste
2 ounces Tabasco Chipotle Sauce
1 ounce Sriracha Hot Chili Sauce
1 pound live steamer clams, cleaned
celery salt, to taste
fresh ground black pepper, to taste

Add the water, vegetable stock, and dashi to a large saucepan over medium-high heat. Stir well and bring to a boil. Then add the roasted tomatoes, diced tomatoes, tomato paste, hot sauce, Sriracha, and clams. Season lightly with celery salt and black pepper. Cover and cook until all the clams open, 3 to 5 minutes. Remove from the heat, discard the clams (you can also eat them), and strain the liquid through a fine strainer, into a container filled with about 2 quarts of ice. Allow the ice to melt, then, if you have a centrifuge, spin the mixture until very clear. Remove and season with salt and pepper again to taste. Transfer to a sealed container and store in the refrigerator until needed.

NOTE

If you do not have a centrifuge, you can store the Clamato Mix in the refrigerator for 24 to 48 hours. It may take several days for the flavors to combine and the solids to settle, meaning it will not be as "fresh" tasting due to the length of time the mixture is sitting unused. Otherwise, you can buy a good used centrifuge online for around $250.

CARROT & PEACH
——— BLOODY MARIA ———

This take on the Bloody Mary comes from Ash Webb, author of the blog spot The Board and Wire. *When summer knocked on Ash's door while he was looking for an interesting cocktail to serve to friends, peaches came to mind. Although most people don't equate peaches with the Rockies, Ash believes there's no finer fruit than the Palisade peach grown in Denver. Along with fresh peaches, Ash substitutes tequila for the vodka to offer a tip of the cap to the thread of Mexican-American culture that runs through the Southwest. What's pleasant about this sweet gem of a drink is that it packs the flavor and heat of a traditional Bloody Mary while the splash of lemon juice keeps the peach from descending into cloying. The garnish is equally spectacular—a sweet, spicy, slightly pickled South African Golden Peppadew filled with cool, butter-soft Gorgonzola Dolce.*

Serves 1

⅔ cup carrot juice
⅓ cup Palisade Peach Nectar (or any thick, pulpy peach nectar)
1 splash tomato juice
1 splash fresh lemon juice
½ teaspoon prepared horseradish, or to taste
½ teaspoon Tabasco Hot Sauce, or to taste
1½ ounces premium tequila, or more
skewered Peppadews filled with Gorgonzola Dolce; peach slice and
fresh cilantro sprig, for garnish

In an ice-filled jar or glass, add the carrot juice, peach nectar (add an extra splash if you love peaches), tomato juice, and lemon juice. Stir in the horseradish and Tabasco. Add the tequila. Garnish and serve.

CHARRED CHILI
——— BLOODY MARIA ———

Summers for a food and lifestyle blogger are synonymous with fun in the garden and the bounty that comes as the season ends. When it's harvest time for chef/mom Kate Ramon, aka Nueva Latina, who shares her take on Latin-inspired food and drink on the site Hola! Jalapeño, *she often finds herself making batch after batch of fresh tomato juice from the ripe tomatoes in her garden. Her fresh juice, with the perfect amount of salt and spice, is great for a refreshing Bloody made with tequila. These two ingredients complement each other so well, especially when you spice it up with a charred chili, as you'll find in this tasty concoction. Of course, if you don't have an abundance of ripe tomatoes at your disposal, or don't want to go through the trouble of making your own juice (we included the recipe anyway), a high-quality store-bought tomato juice is perfectly acceptable.*

Serves 1

Rim
lemon juice
kosher salt
celery salt

2 ounces Charred Chili-Infused
Tequila, recipe on page 44
4 ounces Fresh Tomato Juice, recipe
on page 44

1 tablespoon fresh lemon juice
½ teaspoon horseradish
3 or 4 dashes Worcestershire sauce
3 or 4 dashes hot sauce
1 pinch celery salt
1 pinch fresh ground black pepper
lemon zest, lemon wedge, for garnish

Rim a glass (page 13) with the lemon wedge, kosher salt, and celery salt mixture, and fill the glass with ice.

In a cocktail shaker filled with ice, add the Charred Chili-Infused Tequila, Fresh Tomato Juice, lemon juice, prepared horseradish, Worcestershire sauce, hot sauce, celery salt, and black pepper. Shake well to blend. Strain the cocktail into the prepared glass. Garnish and serve.

CHARRED CHILI-INFUSED TEQUILA

1 fresh jalapeño (or other spicy
    chili), grilled or broiled until the
    skin is charred and blistered
1 bottle (375ml) premium tequila

Add the charred chili to the tequila
bottle and let sit at least 1 hour or up
to 1 week, depending on how spicy
you like your tequila. The longer it
sits, the spicier it gets.

FRESH TOMATO JUICE

Makes about 1 quart

2 pounds very ripe tomatoes (about
    4 large), cored and quartered
1 stalk celery with leaves
1 large handful fresh Italian (flat-
    leaf) parsley
½ small red onion, peeled and
    quartered
2 or 3 dashes hot sauce
¼ teaspoon kosher salt

Add the tomatoes, celery, Italian
parsley, and red onion through a juicer
or purée in a blender until liquefied.
Whisk in the hot sauce and salt. Cover
and refrigerate for up to 3 days.

FIRE-ROASTED GREEN ———— BLOODY MARIA ————

Growing up, Dane Nakamura of Bryan Voltaggio's VOLT Restaurant in Frederick, Maryland, remembers grilling green tomatoes over a hickory fire all summer long. Green tomatoes have a natural tart acidity that absorbs the smoky goodness from the wood-fired grill, which is the inspiration behind this delicious cocktail. Yellow tomatoes, also used, are sweet, have all of that umami goodness, and luckily keep pretty neutral when it comes to coloring the final drink. Celery juice is the key to seasoning the mix while the cucumber adds body and makes the flavor of the mix refreshing. Instead of traditional Worcestershire, Dane uses shiro dashi. It has a finer, smokier flavor while delivering that savory umami punch. The spice from the jalapeños lingers and warms the drink. It's not shocking, just consistently present. Without question, the fresh seasonings in this Bloody Maria are simple and lend themselves well to combining with gin, mezcal, or tequila. But because of the charred characteristics, this beverage is also great with bourbon, rye, or even Irish whiskey.

Serves 1

Rim
sea salt
lime zest

2 ounces spirit (gin, mezcal, tequila, bourbon, rye or Irish whiskey)
5 to 6 ounces Fire-Roasted Green Bloody Maria Mix, recipe on page 46
pickled vegetables, goat cheese fritters, pickles, olives, citrus wedges, for garnish

Rim a tall vessel (page 13) with the sea salt and lime zest, and fill the glass with ice. Add the desired spirit and Fire-Roasted Green Bloody Maria Mix. Stir well using a long-handled bar spoon. Garnish and serve.

FIRE-ROASTED GREEN BLOODY MARIA MIX

3 green tomatoes
½ yellow onion, peeled
1 jalapeño
2 lemons
3 cloves garlic, whole and unpeeled
2 large yellow tomatoes
2 stalks celery, with leaves
1 cucumber

½ cup water
1 teaspoon soy sauce
1 tablespoon shiro dashi
1 cup fresh cilantro leaves, loosely packed
1 cup fresh basil leaves, loosely packed
sea salt and black pepper, to taste

Prepare an outdoor grill using hickory wood (or hickory-flavored charcoal). Hickory lends an extra depth of smoky flavor that allows it to work with different spirits.

Halve the green tomatoes, onion, jalapeño, and lemons. If you prefer a spicier Bloody Maria, leave the seeds in the jalapeño. Arrange the tomatoes, onion, jalapeño and lemon halves on the grill. Add the garlic on the outside of the grill. Grill until the vegetables are cooked and blistered but not burned, about 5 to 7 minutes. Remove from heat and immediately transfer the grilled vegetables into a large ziptop bag. Seal tightly, and set aside.

Next, dice the yellow tomatoes, celery, and cucumber. Add to a blender along with the water, soy sauce, shiro dashi, cilantro, and basil. Blend until smooth. Season with salt and pepper. Open the ziptop bag and remove the grilled lemon halves. Squeeze the juice into the blender, and discard the rinds. Add the grilled green tomatoes, onion, and jalapeño. Season again with salt and pepper and a little more lemon juice, if necessary. Blend until puréed. Strain through a fine mesh sieve. Refrigerate until ready to use.

—— HOLY GUAC-A-MARIA ——

FIG restaurant in Santa Monica, California, is a seasonally inspired kitchen located inside the gates of the Fairmont Miramar Hotel & Bungalows. A stroll through this relaxing poolside hideaway and into the bustling kitchen reveals master chefs and mixologists at work creating flavorful but not over-the-top New American dishes and drinks with a Mediterranean flair. When FIG introduced their full taco bar during their weekend brunch, they needed a refreshing and memorable cocktail to accompany the culinary venue. Meet the Holy Guac-a-Maria. This lighter version of the traditional Bloody Maria is green in color and pairs exceptionally well with a side of tomatillo braised lengua (tongue) tacos. Too much? We don't think so.

Serves 1

2 ounces premium tequila (Casa Noble Silver)
4 ounces Tomatillo Salsa, recipe follows
tomatillo wheel, for garnish

In a Collins glass, add the tequila and top with crushed ice. Add the Tomatillo Salsa and stir well. Garnish and serve.

TOMATILLO SALSA

2 fresh tomatillos, peeled
1 jalapeño
2 garlic cloves, peeled
1 fresh bunch cilantro
2½ limes, juiced
6 ounces water
¼ ripe avocado, peeled and pitted

In a blender, add the tomatillos, jalapeño, garlic, cilantro, lime juice, and water. Blend well until combined. Strain through a chinois and return the strained mixture back into the blender. Slowly blend in the avocado. Refrigerate until ready to use.

JOHNNY MAC'S
—— BLOODY MARIA ——

This tasty Bloody Maria is the creation of John McCarthy, a notable mixologist from New York. When approached by a dear friend who was opening a hip cantina called Masa y Agave, John went to work designing a special cocktail for the establishment. At the time, John had been experimenting with infusing blanco tequila and grilling a variety of garnishes. As a result, this beauty was born, capturing the essence of the cantina.

Serves 1

Rim
Ancho Chili Salt, recipe follows

2 ounces Jalapeño & Serrano Chili-Infused Blanco Tequila, recipe on page 50
4 ounces Bloody Maria Mix, recipe on page 50
roasted corn slice or wheel, habañero-pickled red onion,
half roasted jalapeño, for garnish

Rim a glass (page 13) with the Ancho Chili Salt, and fill the glass with ice. Add the Jalapeño & Serrano Chili-Infused Blanco Tequila and Bloody Maria Mix. Stir well. Garnish and serve.

ANCHO CHILI SALT

1 dried ancho chili, de-stemmed
sea salt, as needed

Using a mortar with pestle, grind the ancho chili until finely broken. Add an equal amount of sea salt and grind until smooth.

JALAPEÑO & SERRANO CHILI–INFUSED BLANCO TEQUILA

Makes 1 liter

1 fresh jalapeño
1 fresh Serrano chili
1 liter blanco tequila (Pueblo Viejo)

Remove the stems from the jalapeño and Serrano chili, and cut lengthwise into four segments each. Place the segments, including pith and seeds, into a 1-liter bottle of blanco tequila, and let macerate overnight. The next day, strain the now infused tequila, discarding the solids, and place the liquid back into the bottle. Store until ready to use.

BLOODY MARIA MIX

Makes about ¾ liter

23 ounces canned tomato juice
1 ounce fresh lime juice
1 ounce olive brine
6 tablespoons prepared horseradish
2 tablespoons Worcestershire sauce
6 dashes Tabasco Hot Sauce
1 teaspoon salt
1 teaspoon coarse ground
    black pepper
1 teaspoon celery salt
½ teaspoon celery seed

In a pitcher or suitable container, add the tomato juice, lime juice, olive brine, prepared horseradish, Worcestershire sauce, hot sauce, salt, black pepper, celery salt, and celery seed. Stir until blended, and let macerate overnight in the refrigerator. Will keep up to 1 week.

ROGELIO MARIA

Good friend and cocktail aficionado Roger Ebner, who provides us with the refreshing Cozy Cove Michelada recipe (page 157), offers this savory cocktail from his coveted Bloody Mary archives. This beverage includes an ingredient not often associated with a Bloody Mary— Maggie Jugo, a salty roasted-flavored seasoning sauce from Mexico, available at most Latin markets.

Serves 1

Seasoned Rim
Lime juice
Celery salt
Seasoned salt (preferably Lawry's)

1 fresh lime, juiced
1½ ounces premium silver tequila
1 tablespoon Worcestershire sauce
1 or 2 dashes Maggie Jugo Seasoning Sauce
Tabasco Hot Sauce, to taste
Bloody Mary mix, recipe on page 33
lime wedge, for garnish

Rim a tall glass (page 13) with the celery salt and seasoned salt, and fill the glass with ice. Add the lime juice (an important ingredient, so don't skimp), along with the tequila, Worcestershire sauce, and Maggie Jugo. Add the heat with hot sauce to your tolerability. Top off with your favorite Bloody Mary mix (or choose one from the collection of mixes in this book). Stir vigorously. Garnish and serve.

BLOODY MIRIAM

Pascal Attar of Ya Hala Lebanese Cuisine in Portland, Oregon, offers a twist on the original Red Snapper Bloody Mary (page 25) by incorporating spicy Middle Eastern flavors you would normally find in Lebanese dishes with the classic staples like horseradish and Tabasco. What also sets this cocktail apart is a sliced garnish of basturma, an Anatolian cured meat. Introduced in the spring of 2015, the Bloody Miriam is rich with more than tomato, so expect a full flavor profile with a rustic culture coming through with every sip.

Serves 1

Rim
kosher salt
Aleppo pepper

½ ounce fresh lime juice
1½ ounces premium vodka
Ya Hala Signature Bloody Mary Mix,
recipe on page 53

1 (6-inch) skewer with a thin
slice of basturma (or substitute
with another cured meat), cucumber
slice, pickled cauliflower, pickled
turnip, cherry tomato, and Kalamata
olive, for garnish

Rim a chilled 16-ounce pint glass (page 13) with salt and Aleppo pepper, and fill the glass with ice. Add the lime juice and vodka. Fill the rest of the glass with Ya Hala Bloody Mary Mix. Garnish and serve.

YA HALA SIGNATURE BLOODY MARY MIX

Makes about ½ liter

½ liter tomato juice
½ teaspoon fresh ground black pepper
½ teaspoon kosher salt
½ teaspoon Aleppo pepper
½ teaspoon sumac
1 teaspoon dried garlic powder
1½ teaspoon cumin
½ teaspoon Ras el Hanout
½ teaspoon allspice
¼ ounce Tabasco Hot Sauce
2 tablespoons Worcestershire sauce
2 tablespoons Moroccan Harissa
2 tablespoons prepared horseradish

In a large, sealable container, combine the tomato juice, black pepper, kosher salt, Aleppo pepper, sumac, dried garlic powder, cumin, Ras el Hanout, allspice, hot sauce, Worcestershire sauce, Moroccan Harissa, and prepared horseradish. Mix well, and place the container in the refrigerator for 24 hours, then strain finely through cheesecloth.

In this chapter . . .

COLORFUL MARYS

During those long, hot summer days, cool down with a flavorful and refreshing Bloody Mary from the creative collection of bloodies featured in this chapter. Although these cocktails can be served year-round, they're best in the summer when you can enhance the flavor of the drink with the natural sweetness of ripe fruit or the crispness of vegetables plucked fresh from the garden. Colorful Bloody Marys like the Blackberry Mary, the Carrot Bloody Mary, the Chelsea Green Mary, the Key West Yellow Mary, and the Watermelon Bloody Mary all incorporate fresh ingredients that add color and variety to the cocktail, while elevating each drink to a higher standard. When purchasing fresh herbs, fruits, and vegetables for these delicious Bloody Marys, be selective. Choose ingredients that have good color, are ripe, and are free from bruises and blemishes, particularly fruit. For juices, whenever possible, buy fresh and not canned, frozen, or from concentrate. Or hand-squeeze the juice yourself. Making homemade tomato juice or a Bloody Mary mix may seem more labor intensive, but the final result is well worth the effort. You may also want to try substituting tomato juice for tomato water for a much lighter Bloody Mary, like featured in the Bloodless House Bloody Mary, the Gnarly Tomato Water Bloody Mary, or the Sunny Mary. The spirit spectrum also broadens. In the previous chapter, the common liquor is vodka, gin, and tequila. In the recipes ahead, rum, rye, scotch, wine, and even Aquavit and moonshine make an appearance, along with a variety of liquor infusions, which incorporate a wide array of ingredients, from jalapeño and tomatillo, to bacon and smoked salmon. The Bloody Mary mixes and purées are equally diverse, so get ready for a new take on the Bloody Mary.

7452 MARY

From the historic New York hotel that brought us the original Bloody Mary (page 25), The St. Regis's Utah location has a signature Bloody Mary of its own. Perched at 7,452 feet in Deer Valley, The St. Regis Deer Valley Hotel serves the 7452 Mary with black lava salt to honor the silver miners who founded Park City many years ago, along with cayenne pepper and a wasabi and celery espuma foam. The foam contributes to the smoothness and complexity of this drink while the presentation leaves guests with a memorable experience.

Serves 1

Rim
black lava salt

1 ounce premium vodka (Vodka 7000, High West Distillery)
1 dash fresh lemon juice
2 ounces tomato juice
2 dashes fresh ground black pepper
2 dashes celery salt
3 dashes Worcestershire sauce
Wasabi-Celery Espuma Foam, recipe on page 58
2 dashes cayenne pepper

Rim a wine glass (page 13) with black lava salt, and fill the glass with ice.

In a mixing glass filled with ice, add the vodka, lemon juice, tomato juice, black pepper, celery salt, and Worcestershire sauce. Stir well to combine. Pour into the prepared glass. Layer the Wasabi-Celery Espuma Foam on top and sprinkle with cayenne pepper.

WASABI-CELERY ESPUMA FOAM

48 ounces celery juice
24 ounces green apple juice
3 tablespoons wasabi powder
1 tablespoon salt
2 teaspoons Xantana
3 limes, juiced
1 fresh bunch fresh Italian (flat-leaf) parsley, leaves only

In a blender, add the celery juice, green apple juice, wasabi powder, salt, Xantana, lime juice, and Italian parsley. Blend together until pureéd. Fine-strain the liquid and add to the prepared glass using the cream whipper.

NOTE

This recipe yields enough to fill a stainless steel cream whipper and fill multiple drinks. The whipper is available at kitchen stores or online for $50 to $60. Meanwhile, Xantana is a dried product that comes from the fermentation of cornstarch with the same bacteria found in cabbage. The result is a gum with great thickening power. For this recipe, the addition of Xantana allows the foam to remain suspended on top. Without it, the foam would sink into the cocktail.

—BACON JAM BLOODY MARY—

This recipe is courtesy of Skillet in Seattle, Washington. Before establishing the restaurant, Skillet was a food truck, and the first in Seattle, cruising around town in a chrome vintage Airstream trailer. Today, the thriving eatery features house-made bacon jam throughout their menu, including in their signature Bacon Jam Bloody Mary. The bacon jam—a spreadable bacon condiment—is really the secret weapon here, which is infused into the vodka, while the House-Made Bloody Mary Mix balances perfectly with the bacon jam vodka infusion to add heat and smoke. It's all finished with a perfect rim comprising of bacon, salt, smoked paprika, hickory smoke powder (available online), and chipotle powder to set the whole thing over the top for any bacon lover.

Both Skillet's Original Bacon Jam and Bacon Salt are available online at: www. skilletfood.com. If you prefer making your own, we attempted to replicate the recipes below.

Serves 1

Rim
Bacon Salt Rim

Canadian bacon, cooked and finely minced
salt
smoked paprika
Hickory smoke powder
chipotle powder
2 ounces Bacon Jam Vodka, recipe on page 60
6 ounces House-Made Bloody Mary Mix, recipe on page 60
celery, pickle, hot pepper, olive, lemon, and lime, for garnish

On a saucer or plate, combine equal parts minced bacon, salt, smoked paprika, hickory smoke powder, and chipotle powder. Rim a 16-ounce glass or Mason jar (page 13) with the Bacon Salt and fill the glass with ice. Add the Bacon Jam Vodka and House-Made Bloody Mary Mix. Stir well to combine. Garnish and serve.

BACON JAM

1 part balsamic vinegar
1 part brown sugar
1 part bacon, finely minced
1 part onion, finely minced
salt and black pepper, to taste

Slowly heat equal parts balsamic vinegar, brown sugar, minced bacon, and minced onion in a saucepan over low heat. Slowly cook until the onions are caramelized and the bacon is rendered. Remove from heat and let cool. Season with salt and black pepper.

BACON JAM-INFUSED VODKA

4 tablespoons Bacon Jam (see previous recipe)
1 bottle (750ml) vodka

In a small skillet over low heat, add the bacon spread and warm. Remove from heat and strain into the vodka. Seal the bottle and store in a cold, dark place for 48 hours. Using a coffee filter or cheesecloth, strain the vodka into another bottle, discarding the bacon spread. Seal and store until needed.

HOUSE-MADE BLOODY MARY MIX

Makes approximately 6 ounces (1 cocktail)

3½ ounces tomato juice
½ ounce Worcestershire sauce
½ lemon, juiced
½ ounce prepared horseradish
⅛ ounce olive brine
⅛ tablespoon muddled capers
1 dash Sriracha Hot Chili Sauce
1 dash ground chipotle pepper
1 dash fresh ground black pepper
1 dash celery salt

In a suitable glass or container, add the tomato juice, Worcestershire sauce, lemon juice, prepared horseradish, olive brine, capers, hot sauce, chipotle pepper, black pepper, and celery salt. Mix well to combine.

BRAVEHEART
— A.K.A. SCOTCH BLOODY MARY —

Here's a super simple Bloody Mary from Tim Heuisler at Time Restaurant in Philadelphia. The drink is actually a collaborative effort with two other Philadelphia bartenders, Grant Somerdyk and Jesse Cornell. The trio substitutes traditional vodka for Black Grouse Scotch (available at liquor stores and online) because they like how the smokiness of the scotch plays with the spiciness of a good Bloody Mary mix (the boys prefer McClure's, available online, because it's briny and spicy). They never put the Braveheart on the menu, but the minute they mention the drink, everyone seems to order one. Just be careful—a couple of these and you'll be standing up and yelling, "Freedom!"

Serves 1

2 ounces premium scotch (Black Grouse)
3½ ounces Bloody Mary mix (McClure's)
½ ounce fresh lemon juice
½ ounce Worcestershire sauce
1 pinch celery salt
1 pinch fresh grated horseradish
gherkin, pickled onion, bacon strip, for garnish

In a cocktail shaker filled with ice, add the scotch, Bloody Mary mix, lemon juice, Worcestershire sauce, celery salt, and horseradish. Shake well and strain into an ice-filled glass. Garnish and serve.

—ALASKAN SOCKEYE MARY—

Nothing is more Alaskan than smoked Copper River sockeye salmon. Wild caught and sustainably harvested, these 100 percent nature-as-God-intended fish represent one of the most exquisite proteins we can put in our body. Mix it with water melted down from icebergs hand-harvested from tidewater glaciers, and you have one of the most unique vodkas in the world. Dorene M. Lorenz of Alaska Distillery in Wasilla, Alaska, admits it took forty-seven attempts to get it right, but their Alaska Distillery Sockeye Smoked Salmon Vodka is definitely extraordinary (and available online). What you will find is an underlying soft smoky sweet meat flavor with a smooth finish. For those who are adventurous enough to give this Alaskan Sockeye Mary a try, you may never settle for any other vodka in your Bloody Mary again.

Serves 1

4–6 ounces tomato juice
1 teaspoon fresh grated horseradish
4 splashes Tabasco Hot Sauce
2 ounces Alaska Distillery Sockeye Smoked Salmon Vodka
1 ounce Clamato juice (or trying making your own, page 39)
1 teaspoon lime juice
1 pinch Old Bay Seasoning
1 pinch celery salt
Worcestershire sauce, to taste
fresh ground black pepper, to taste
olives, Alaska smoked salmon, Dungeness or King Crab leg, for garnish

In a cocktail shaker filled with ice, add the tomato juice, horseradish, hot sauce, vodka, Clamato juice, lime juice, Old Bay Seasoning, celery salt, Worcestershire sauce, and black pepper. Shake well and pour into an ice-filled glass. Garnish and serve.

── BEETNIK BLOODY MARY ──

Here's a Bloody Mary with an earthy tone and a bold fuchsia-purple hue, complements of Mac Hansen, general manager at Seattle's Hattie's Hat. Hattie's Hat, incidentally, is a time-honored Seattle institution, considered a relic from Old Ballard, Seattle's historic maritime neighborhood established in 1904, which is cherished as much for its architectural history as for its eclectic twist on comfort food and cocktails. Because many of the menu items feature farm-fresh beets delivered weekly, the bountiful, beautiful beets used in this Bloody Mary offer splendid color as well as nutrition.

Serves 1

Rim
lime wedge
kosher salt

3 ounces Beet-Infused Vodka, recipe on page 66
½ ounce fresh lime juice
3 ounces Hattie's Hat Bloody Mary Mix, recipe on page 66
skewer of pickled okra, red onion, lemon wedge, olive, and pepperoncini
pepper, for garnish

Rim a glass (page 13) with the kosher salt, and fill the glass with ice.

In a cocktail shaker filled with ice, add the Beet-Infused Vodka, lime juice, and Hattie's Hat Bloody Mary Mix. Shake well and pour into the prepared glass. Garnish and serve.

BEET-INFUSED VODKA

Makes 1 liter

1 fresh beet, chopped into cubes
1 liter vodka

In a container, add the chopped beets
and vodka (note: to make more, use 1
beet per liter of vodka). Seal and store
in a dark cold place for 5 to 7 days.
Stir and taste on the third day. Using
a coffee filter or cheesecloth, strain
the vodka into a bottle or container,
discarding the beets. Seal and store
until needed.

HATTIE'S HAT BLOODY MARY MIX

Makes about 1 quart

3 cups tomato juice
3 tablespoons fresh lemon juice
1 tablespoon horseradish, fresh grated
1 tablespoon Worcestershire sauce
1 teaspoon minced garlic
¾ teaspoon salt
½ teaspoon fresh ground black pepper

In a container, combine the tomato
juice, lemon juice, horseradish,
Worcestershire sauce, garlic, salt, and
black pepper. Mix well and chill in the
refrigerator for at least 2 hours before
serving.

BLACKBERRY MARY

Mixologist Terence Mooney of the former W Hotel in San Diego, California, admits this particular cocktail is a crowd pleaser because it is beautiful, delicious . . . and unexpected. And rightfully so. The Blackberry Mary is the perfect marriage of sweet and spicy that will appeal to the Bloody Mary novice and connoisseur alike. Although it may look sweet and innocent, the Blackberry Mary has a kick, thanks to fresh jalapeño slices and Stoli Hot Jalapeño-Flavored Vodka, which is available at liquor stores and online (or try making your own jalapeño-vodka infusion; page 97).

Serves 1

Rim
kosher salt

4–5 fresh blackberries
½ ounce fresh lime juice
½ ounce fresh lemon juice
½ ounce Chili Syrup, recipe on page 68
2 fresh jalapeño slices
1½ ounces Stoli Hot Jalapeño-Flavored Vodka
3 ounces House Bloody Mary Mix, recipe on page 68
jalapeño slice, cucumber rounds, blackberries, for garnish

Rim a wine or martini glass (page 13) with the kosher salt.

In a cocktail shaker, add the blackberries, lime juice, lemon juice, chili syrup, and jalapeño slices and muddle aggressively. Add the vodka, some ice, and the House Bloody Mary Mix. Shake and strain into the prepared glass. Garnish and serve.

CHILI SYRUP

Makes about 3/4 cup

1 cup water
1 cup sugar
1 fresh jalapeño, sliced lengthwise

In a saucepan over medium-high heat, add the water and sugar. Stir until the sugar dissolves and the liquid is clear. Add the sliced jalapeño. Bring to a simmer, and reduce the heat to low. Cook for 12 minutes, keeping a watchful eye that it doesn't boil. Remove from heat, cover, and let steep for 10 minutes. Strain and let cool. Transfer to a Mason jar or suitable container. Seal tightly and store in refrigerator for up to 2 weeks.

HOUSE BLOODY MARY MIX

3 cups (24 ounces) tomato juice
1½ ounces fresh lemon juice
1½ ounces fresh lime juice
1 tablespoon Worcestershire sauce
1 teaspoon horseradish, finely grated
1½ teaspoons kosher salt
1 teaspoon Tabasco Hot Sauce
1 teaspoon celery salt
¾ teaspoon fresh ground black pepper

In a pitcher or suitable container, add the tomato juice, lemon juice, lime juice, Worcestershire sauce, horseradish, kosher salt, hot sauce, celery salt, and black pepper. Mix well to combine and refrigerate until ready to use.

BLOODLESS HOUSE ——— BLOODY MARY ———

Josh Goldman of Belcampo Meat Company in Santa Monica admits he doesn't like the texture of tomato juice. What he has perfected here is a Bloody Mary that is more refined without altering the overall flavor profile or completely changing what is the essence of a Bloody Mary. Of course, serving a Bloody Mary at a meat company means there must be a meat component to the drink, and there is. Josh adds bacon to this rum-based concoction—twice. Although the recipe may seem long and potentially daunting, do not be alarmed. Josh crafted this Bloody Mary to be an easy build once the prep work is done so they can be served to customers fast—because nobody likes to wait for a Bloody when they really need one.

Serves 1

2 ounces Bacon & Black Pepper Vodka, recipe on page 72
1 ounce fresh lemon juice, strained
4 ounces Clarified Tomato Water, recipe on page 72
4 drops House-Made Spicy Tincture, recipe on page 73 (can also use store-bought)
1 Celery Ice Cube, recipe on page 73
lemon wedge, Candied Bacon, recipe on page 74 (can also use store-bought), edible
flowers, for garnish

In a cocktail shaker filled with ice, add the Bacon & Black Pepper Vodka, lemon juice, Clarified Tomato Water, and House-Made Spicy Tincture. Shake, and finely strain into a pilsner glass with the Celery Ice Cube. Garnish and serve.

BACON & BLACK PEPPER VODKA

Makes about 1 liter

1 teaspoon mushroom powder, divided
2 teaspoons fresh ground black pepper, divided
1 (750-ml) bottle vodka, divided
4 strips cooked bacon
4 strips raw bacon

Add ½ teaspoon of the mushroom powder and 1 teaspoon of the black pepper into a Cryovac vacuum bag (available online). Add the remaining mushroom powder and black pepper into a second bag. Next, add half the vodka to each bag. Add all the cooked bacon into one bag and the uncooked bacon into the other bag. Seal both bags and circulate them in a hot 165°F water bath for 2 hours. Open both bags and strain the liquid into a suitable size container, seal and freeze overnight. Remove the container from the freezer and strain through wet coffee filters into the empty vodka bottle or other suitable size container.

CLARIFIED TOMATO WATER

Volume varies, depending on how much you would like to make[*]

fresh tomatoes
1 percent white sugar
1 percent kosher salt

Rough chop the tomatoes and add to an electric blender. Blend into a purée. Pour into a saucepot and stir in the 1 percent sugar and 1 percent salt (by volume). Place over medium heat and bring to a boil. Once boiling, skim off the solids floating on top with a slotted spoon. Once all the solids are removed, you should be left with only liquid. Remove from heat and strain through a chinois lined with wet coffee filters. Refrigerate until ready to use, or freeze for use later.

---

[*]Example: If you'd like to make 1 gallon of Clarified Tomato Water (128 ounces), you'd use 1 gallon of tomato purée (128 ounces), 1.25 ounces kosher salt, and 1.25 ounces white sugar.

NOTE

If you don't have access to Cryovac vacuum bags, you can simply render the fat out of the bacon, and pour the bacon fat into the vodka (at a ratio of 50 ml of bacon fat per one 750ml bottle of vodka). You can also use a Mason jar to combine all the ingredients, shake well, and let sit for 6 to 12 hours before freezing. Then strain through wet coffee filters into the empty vodka bottle or other suitable size container.

HOUSE-MADE SPICY TINCTURE

Makes about 750ml

4 fresh jalapeños
4 fresh Serrano chilies
2 fresh habañero chilies
2 fresh Thai birdseye chilies
1 bottle (750ml) J Wray & Nephew
    White Overproof Rum

Remove the stems from the chilies and rough chop. Add the chopped peppers into a Cryovac vacuum bag (available online). Next, add the rum. Seal the bag and circulate in a hot 120°F water bath for 4 hours. Open the bag and strain the liquid back into the empty rum bottle or other suitable size container, seal, and store until ready to use.

CELERY ICE CUBES

Quantity varies, depending on size and how many you would like to make

1 or more bunches fresh celery

In a large bowl, prepare an ice bath (simply water and ice).

Boil a large pot of water over the stove. Add the celery and boil for 1 to 2 minutes (celery should turn bright green). Quickly strain and add the blanched celery to the ice water bath to stop the cooking process. Remove the celery, and dry with paper towels. Run the celery through a juicer or blender until liquefied. Strain the juice into ice cube molds or trays, and freeze 24 to 48 hours before using.

NOTE

You can also buy a spicy tincture like Bitterman's Hellfire Habañero Shrub or Scrappy's Firewater Bitters. If you would still like to make your own tincture, and don't have access to Cryovac vacuum bags, simply pour all the ingredients into a Mason jar, seal tightly, and check after 48 hours. You can let the tincture sit up to 1 week depending on the desired heat level you're trying to achieve.

BACON CANDY

Makes 25–30 pieces

12 slices bacon (less fat the better)
½ cup Demerara sugar
2 teaspoons fresh ground black pepper

Preheat the oven to 325°F.

Add the bacon slices into a large bowl. Add the sugar and black pepper. Toss well to combine.

Line a baking sheet with parchment paper and arrange the bacon in a single layer. Sprinkle any sugar and pepper left in the bowl over the bacon. Top the bacon with another layer of parchment paper and cover, squarely, with another baking sheet.

Place the tray in the center of the oven and bake for 20 minutes. Check the bacon by lifting the top tray and parchment. If the bacon is not golden brown and fairly crispy, cook for an additional 10 to 15 minutes. The trick is to be patient and do not turn up the oven. The bacon will continue to crisp as it cools down after removing from the oven.

After the bacon has cooled, cut into 3-inch pieces and store between wax paper in an airtight container with some silica gel packs. Store until ready to use.

—— BLOODY WHITE PEACH ——

Artisan cocktails with fresh, local ingredients are more popular than ever. For Elizabeth Dodder, lifestyle and food blogger for FoodCharmer.com, this couldn't ring more true. During a recent summer outing at a California winery, she found herself sipping a tomato-hot pepper-peach-white wine cocktail. Not long after, when visiting family and friends in Georgia, she came across ripe peaches and cherry tomatoes from a local garden. In the high heat and humidity of a typical southern afternoon, Elizabeth had the idea to combine fresh tomato juice with muddled peaches, along with some lime, simple syrup, cilantro, and Sauvignon Blanc. The result is this riff on the Bloody Mary.

Serves 2

---

1 tablespoon fresh cilantro leaves, chopped
8 vine-ripe cherry tomatoes
1 small farm-fresh peach, pitted, skinned and chopped
1 lime, juiced
2 teaspoons simple syrup (or more to taste)
8 ounces Dry Sauvignon Blanc, very chilled
splash sparkling water or soda (optional)
fresh cilantro leaves, for garnish

In a cocktail shaker or mixing glass, add the cilantro, tomatoes, peach, lime juice, and simple syrup. Muddle until well combined. Strain into two large chilled glasses filled with some ice (note: it's okay if some of the fruit falls into the glass, but try to avoid any seeds or skin). Top each glass with wine (about 4 ounces per glass), and stir. For more of a bubbly, spritzer cocktail, add a splash of soda water. Garnish and serve.

— CAPRESE BLOODY MARY —

At Olive and June's in Austin, Texas, they adore the Bloody Mary, which is why they decided to add their own twist on the classic beverage. Because their fresh caprese salad is always so delicious, they fused the two. The herbaceous character of this cocktail is really what shines, leaning very aromatic on the nose, while the touch of balsamic is super savory on the palate.

Serves 1

1½ ounces Basil Bloom–Infused Vodka, recipe on opposite page
2 teaspoons Basil Simple Syrup, recipe on opposite page
3 dashes celery salt
3 dashes fresh ground black pepper
3 dashes Tabasco Hot Sauce
¾ ounce fresh lemon juice
¾ ounce olive juice
½ ounce premium aged balsamic vinegar
tomato juice, as needed
skewer of cherry tomato, mozzarella ball, and basil leaf, drizzled with balsamic vinegar, for garnish

Fill a Collins glass with ice, and add the Basil Bloom–Infused Vodka, Basil Simple Syrup, celery salt, black pepper, hot sauce, lemon juice, olive juice, and balsamic vinegar. Stir well with a long-handled bar spoon and top off with tomato juice. Garnish and serve.

BASIL BLOOM–INFUSED VODKA

1 bunch fresh basil, washed and dried
1 bottle (1½ liters) vodka (Titos)

Place the basil in the bottom of a clean glass infusion jar, preferably a 1-quart Mason jar. Pour the vodka over the leaves, making sure all the basil is submerged. Seal jar tightly and store in a cool, dark place for at least 24 hours, but not more than 72 hours. Shake gently once a day, and taste if desired to check progress. Strain through coffee filters into a sealable bottle. Store in the freezer until ready to use.

BASIL SIMPLE SYRUP

1 part water
1 part sugar
1 handful fresh basil leaves, torn to
   release aroma

Heat the water in a small saucepot over medium-high heat until almost boiling. Add the sugar and dissolve. Add the basil, and let steep for 1 hour. Strain into a sealable bottle and store in refrigerator until ready to use.

—— CARROT BLOODY MARY ——

Jonathan Melendez is a cook, baker, blogger, and lucky enough to visit New Orleans on numerous occasions. He tells us the first thing he does before eating the amazing Cajun food, sightseeing, and listening to the super talented street performers is get a Bloody Mary. When it was time for him to prepare a Sunday Brunch for his mother, whose favorite juice is carrot juice, Jonathan's obsession with the Bloody Mary inspired him to create this attractive and delicious cocktail.

Serves 4–6

Rim
lemon juice
celery salt
Old Bay seasoning

7½ ounces premium vodka (or more, depending on your mood)
Carrot Bloody Mary Mix, recipe on opposite page
celery sticks, baby carrots, pickled green beans, pickled onions,
olives, lime wedges, for garnish

Rim some tall glasses (page 13) with the celery salt and Old Bay seasoning mixture, then fill the glasses with ice. Add the vodka and top off each drink with the Carrot Bloody Mary Mix. Garnish and serve.

CARROT BLOODY MARY MIX

48 ounces fresh carrot juice
3 tablespoons prepared horseradish
2 tablespoons fresh lemon juice
2 tablespoons fresh lime juice
1 tablespoon dill pickle juice
10–15 dashes Tabasco Hot Sauce
2 tablespoons Worcestershire sauce
½ teaspoon celery salt
¼ teaspoon salt
¼ teaspoon fresh ground black pepper
2 teaspoons Old Bay Seasoning

In a large pitcher, combine the carrot juice, prepared horseradish, lemon juice, lime juice, pickle juice, hot sauce, Worcestershire sauce, celery salt, salt, black pepper, and Old Bay seasoning. Whisk until evenly combined. Cover with plastic wrap and place in the refrigerator. Chill for at least 1 hour or overnight. Shake well once again before using. Note: The longer the mixture sits and chills, the better the base will taste.

CHARLESTON REAPER
—— BLOODY MARY ——

Charleston is synonymous with Southern hospitality and lazy weekend brunches, and this cocktail is ideal for those dining experiences, but don't let this drink fool you. Anthony Melias of Crave Kitchen in Mount Pleasant, South Carolina, offers a scorching recipe by embracing two bountiful ingredients grown in town, famous yellow tomatoes, and one of the world's hottest peppers, the Carolina Reaper. This pepper is a hybrid between a ghost pepper and a red habañero, which the Guinness Book of World Records *rated as the hottest pepper in the world in 2013.*

Serves 1

Rim
lime juice
crushed red pepper
Old Bay seasoning

1½ ounces Carolina Reaper Pepper Vodka, recipe on page 82
3 or 4 ounces Yellow Tomato Mary Mix, recipe on page 82
2 dashes Angostura Bitters
lime wheel and two small fresh cut palm leaves, for garnish

Rim a glass (page 13) with the crushed red pepper and Old Bay seasoning mixture, and fill the glass with ice. Add the Carolina Reaper Pepper Vodka (or another pepper-flavored vodka from this book). Top with the Yellow Tomato Mary Mix. Add the Angostura Bitters and stir well. Garnish and serve.

81

CAROLINA REAPER PEPPER VODKA

1 bottle (750 fluid ounces) vodka or neutral spirit

½ Carolina Reaper pepper (or substitute with 1 habañero, ghost, scotch bonnet or Trinidad scorpion pepper), quartered

In a Mason jar or suitable glass container, add the vodka, along with the pepper. Seal tightly and let steep for 24 hours. Remove the pepper and strain. If you prefer the vodka to be hotter, leave the pepper in for another day or two (not suggested).

NOTE
Make sure you're wearing gloves when working with the Carolina Reaper pepper.

YELLOW TOMATO MARY MIX

4 medium yellow tomatoes

2 lemons, juiced

1 teaspoon Worcestershire sauce

1 teaspoon Green Tabasco Hot Sauce

1 teaspoon horseradish, finely grated

¾ teaspoon coarse salt

¼ teaspoon fresh ground black pepper

In a blender, add the tomatoes and purée until smooth. Press through a fine sieve into a small bowl, discarding the skins and solids. Stir in the lemon juice, Worcestershire sauce, hot sauce, horseradish, salt, and black pepper. Transfer to a pitcher or suitable container and refrigerate until ready to use.

— CHELSEA GREEN MARY —

A New York City institution for almost fifteen years, Cafeteria serves high-quality American comfort food in a trend-setting, high-energy environment in the heart of Chelsea. And the best part? It's running 24/7, which is perfect for early risers and post-clubbers looking for late-night noshing and creative and refreshing cocktails. Try this beautiful and healthy twist on the iconic Bloody Mary, developed by Cafeteria themselves.

Serves 1

1½ ounces premium vodka
6 ounces Green Mary Base, recipe follows
½ ounce fresh lime juice
3–4 dashes Green Jalapeño Tabasco Hot Sauce
½ teaspoon prepared horseradish

¼ teaspoon celery seed
1 splash olive juice
1 pinch salt
2 turns of the black pepper mill
celery hearts, cucumber slices, lime wedges, green olives, for garnish

In a cocktail shaker filled with ice, add the vodka, Green Mary Base, lime juice, hot sauce, prepared horseradish, celery seed, and olive juice. Shake and strain into a chilled 12-ounce glass. Finish with a pinch of salt and float a few grounds of black pepper on top. Garnish and serve.

GREEN MARY BASE

Makes about 2 cups

1 cup yellow tomatoes, chopped
1 cup tomatillos, husked

½ cup cucumber, peeled and chopped
¼ cup green apple, peeled and chopped

In a blender, add the tomatoes, tomatillos, cucumber, and green apple. Blend until very smooth. Transfer to a sealed container and store in the refrigerator until ready to use.

—— COCONUT CURRY MARY ——

Good friend and mixologist Jennifer Akin of the famed Alchemy Restaurant & Bar in Ashland, Oregon, is a fan of curry. So much so, she enjoys adding the spice to particular cocktails, such as this unique twist on the Bloody Mary. The distinct flavors of the lemongrass, lime, coconut, and kaffir lime leaves marry well together. Add the vodka and you have yourself a wonderful drink with plenty of depth and spice.

Serves 1

---

2 ounces premium vodka
½ ounce fresh lime juice
2–4 dashes Sriracha Hot Chili Sauce
6 ounces Coconut Curry, recipe on page 86
cilantro and cucumber wheel, for garnish

In a glass filled with ice, add the vodka, lime juice, Sriracha, and Coconut Curry. Stir well with a long-handled bar spoon. Garnish and serve.

COCONUT CURRY

1 tablespoon olive oil

1 stalk lemongrass, thinly sliced

1 piece fresh ginger, about 2 inches, peeled and thinly sliced

½ cup yellow onion, peeled and small dice

1 tablespoon salt

½ teaspoon red chili flakes

1 tablespoon curry powder

4 kaffir lime leaves

1 can (about 14 ounces) coconut milk, divided

½ cup water

¼ cup brown sugar

3 limes, zested and juiced

½ bunch fresh cilantro leaves

½ English cucumber, peeled, seeded, and sliced into ¼-inch slices

In a small saucepot, heat the olive oil over low heat. Add the lemongrass, ginger, onion, salt, chili flakes, curry powder, and lime leaves. Stir occasionally, until the onions are translucent, about 5 minutes. Add half the coconut milk and the water. Increase the heat to medium and bring the liquid to a light simmer. Cook for 5 minutes, stirring occasionally. Add the brown sugar and the lime zest and juice, and continue to simmer for 15 minutes. Remove the lime leaves and discard. Transfer the mixture to a blender. Add the remaining coconut milk along with the cilantro. Blend until smooth and cool the mixture in the refrigerator. When cool, add the cucumber to the blender and blend thoroughly. Strain through a fine strainer and store in the refrigerator until ready to use.

DANISH MARY

If you're ever in Portland, Oregon, pay a visit to the Broder Söder Café. Here, you'll enjoy and appreciate the authentic flavors of Nordic Europe. Their signature Danish Mary is handcrafted with Aquavit, a neutral spirit typically distilled from grain and flavored with botanicals. The Nordic spirit is produced in Scandinavia, although you can find quality Aquavits produced in the United States, including several in Portland. The Café's Aquavit is infused with fresh dill to give the cocktail a deeper flavor profile while their Danish Mary Mix is all about the blend of spices. This one's definitely worth a try.

Serves 4

Dill Salt Rim
3 tablespoons kosher salt
1 teaspoon celery salt
1 teaspoon dry dill weed

2 ounces Dill-Infused Aquavit, recipe on page 88
Danish Mary Mix, recipe on page 89
skewer of lemon slices and pickled vegetables of your choice (beets, cucumber, cauliflower, and onion), for garnish

Rim a chilled pint glass (page 13) with the Dill Salt mixture, and fill the glass with ice. Add the Aquavit and top with the Danish Mary Mix (about ½ cup) and gently stir. Garnish and serve.

DILL-INFUSED AQUAVIT

¼ cup coriander seeds
1 (750-ml) bottle premium potato-based vodka (or neutral spirit)
1 bunch fresh dill fronds (preferably from a crown dill, if available)

Use a clean 1-quart-sized Mason glass jar as an infusion vessel. A vodka bottle also works fine, provided your ingredients fit through the small opening. Add the coriander seeds to a small fry pan over low heat, and lightly toast until you smell the aroma, being careful not to burn. Toasting the seeds helps intensify their flavor. Remove from heat and let cool. Add the vodka to the container, along with toasted coriander. Seal tightly and store in a cool, dark place for 1 week. Remove the container and wash the dill thoroughly and dry with paper towels. Open the container and add the dill. Return the container to the cool, dark place for another 3 or 4 days. Remove the container and strain through a coffee filter into a clean container. Seal tightly and store in the freezer until ready to use.

NOTE

For this infusion, a potato vodka works well, such as Chopin or Teton Glacier, which picks up flavors better than grain vodka due to its higher viscosity.

DANISH MARY MIX

Makes about 1½ quarts

1½ teaspoons whole black peppercorns
1 small piece bay leaf
½ teaspoon kosher salt
½ teaspoon dry dill
½ teaspoon white pepper
¼ teaspoon cayenne pepper
½ teaspoon ground cumin
½ teaspoon mustard powder
1 teaspoon celery salt
¼ teaspoon curry powder
½ teaspoon paprika
½ teaspoon coriander
½ teaspoon garlic powder

½ teaspoon onion powder
1 teaspoon brown sugar
½ cup lemon juice
1 tablespoon Worcestershire sauce
1 tablespoon balsamic vinegar
1 tablespoon apple-cider vinegar
1 tablespoon prepared horseradish
⅓ cup tomato paste
46 ounces tomato juice
kosher salt, to taste
fresh ground black pepper, to taste
sugar, to taste

Using a spice grinder, grind the peppercorns, bay leaf, salt, and dry dill.

In a nonstick skillet, add the white pepper, cayenne, cumin, mustard powder, celery salt, curry powder, and paprika. Lightly toast on low heat until fragrant.

In a small bowl, add the coriander, garlic powder, onion powder, and brown sugar. Then add the ground spices and the toasted spice. Mix well to combine all the spices.

In a suitable container, add the spice mixture, along with the lemon juice, Worcestershire sauce, vinegars, prepared horseradish, tomato paste, and tomato juice. Whisk until well incorporated. Taste, and add additional horseradish if needed. Season with salt, pepper, and sugar.

GNARLY TOMATO WATER BLOODY MARY

Like a number of recipes in this book, the Gnarly Tomato Water Bloody Mary is the result of two seemingly unrelated occurrences: an overabundance of one ingredient—in this case tomatoes that were gnarled and sunburned from a brutally hot summer—and a bottle of liquor—here, we're talking about a blazingly hot chili pepper-infused vodka. For blogger Tracey D. Hagan of Salty Sweet Life, nothing makes her happier than cooking for friends and family. Food is her passion, whether she's trying out a new restaurant, delving into a cookbook, or mixing up a cocktail. So when Tracey combines some sweet homemade tomato-water with an over-infused pepper vodka, which she ends up diluting with plain vodka, she finds the result to be a perfect, dragged-through-the-garden Bloody Mary that's refreshing with a tingling heat.

Serves 2

1 pound fresh, ripe tomatoes, sliced
2 teaspoons kosher salt
¼ cup tomato juice
3 tablespoons Hot Pepper-Infused Vodka, recipe on page 92
¼ cup regular vodka
1 teaspoon prepared horseradish, grated
2 tablespoons dill pickle juice
2½ tablespoons fresh lemon juice
2 dashes Worcestershire sauce
2 dashes Tabasco Hot Sauce
1 sprinkle fresh ground black pepper
Thai Basil, cocktail tomato, dill pickle spear, for garnish

Place the fresh, sliced tomatoes in a colander set above a bowl. Sprinkle the tomatoes with the kosher salt and allow the tomatoes to sit for at least one hour. You'll begin to see the water drain from the tomatoes into the bowl. After an hour and just before you prepare the drink, press lightly to squeeze out any additional tomato water. Set the colander of tomatoes aside. Note: don't let the tomatoes go to waste. Use them to make fresh salsa, tomato sauce, or soup.

Pour the collected tomato water into a mixing glass. One pound of tomatoes should yield ½ cup of tomato water. Add the tomato juice, both vodkas, prepared horseradish, pickle juice, lemon juice, Worcestershire sauce, hot sauce, and black pepper to the mixing glass, and stir well.

Pour the cocktail into two tall glasses filled with ice. Garnish and serve.

HOT PEPPER–INFUSED VODKA

1 handful hot peppers (combination of Serrano chilies or jalapeño chilies)
1–2 cups vodka (depending on jar size)

Using a fork, prick the peppers on all sides. Fill a small jar ¾ with the peppers and fill the jar with vodka. Tightly seal the jar, and store in a cool, dark place for 2 days.

HELL MARY

This attractive and award-winning yellow Bloody Mary comes from Arley Howard of the Top of the Hub Restaurant and Lounge in Boston, Massachusetts. Arley's entered this recipe in many contests and competitions and always comes out on top. The Hell Mary was originally named the Hail Mary, like the football pass that's considered a desperate attempt to score without any time left on the clock. But Arley changed the name to Hell Mary to pay homage to the Scotch Bonnet pepper, the sweet cousin of the habañero.

Serves 1

2 ounces premium vodka
4 ounces Yellow Heirloom Tomato Purée, recipe follows
1 ounce Roasted Scotch Bonnet Sauce, recipe on page 94
1½ ounce Raisin Purée, recipe on page 94
Brown Sugared Orange Rind and Turkey Bacon Skewer,
recipe on page 94, for garnish

In a mixing glass, add the vodka, followed by the Yellow Heirloom Tomato Purée, Roasted Scotch Bonnet Sauce, and Raisin Purée in this order. Stir with a bar spoon in a circular motion for 20 seconds. Pour over ice in a 16-ounce highball glass. Garnish and serve.

YELLOW HEIRLOOM TOMATO PURÉE

6½ cups yellow heirloom tomatoes, sliced into quarters
1 cup water
6 ounces kosher salt

In an electric blender, add the tomatoes, water, and kosher salt. Blend until smooth. Store in a sealed container in the refrigerator until ready to use.

ROASTED SCOTCH BONNET SAUCE

2 yellow Scotch Bonnet peppers
extra virgin olive oil, as needed
fine salt, for dusting
8 ounces prepared yellow mustard
2 ounces water
1 teaspoon garlic powder

Preheat the oven to 475°F.

Slice the peppers in half and remove the seeds. Rub or spray the peppers evenly with extra virgin olive oil and place on a baking sheet. Lightly dust the peppers with the salt. Insert the baking sheet into the oven on the middle rack. Roast until the pepper skins are browned, about 15 to 20 minutes. Remove the peppers from the oven, and add to an electric blender or food processor along with the mustard, water, and garlic powder. Blend until liquefied. Store in a sealed container in the refrigerator until ready to use.

RAISIN PURÉE

16 ounces steak sauce (Heinz 57)
6 ounces pitted golden raisins
2 ounces fresh orange juice

In a blender or food processor, add the steak sauce, golden raisins, and orange juice. Blend until puréed. Store in a sealed container in the refrigerator until ready to use.

BROWN SUGARED ORANGE RIND AND TURKEY BACON SKEWER

2 rinds from 2 oranges, sliced into
    ½-inch by 2-inch strips
½ pound organic turkey bacon
½ cup brown sugar
wooden skewer

Separate the rinds from 2 oranges, and cut into the proper size.

Coat a skillet with corn oil and place over medium heat. Add the bacon and orange rinds. Sprinkle the brown sugar into the pan. Cook until the sugar is dissolved into the natural juices of the turkey bacon and the orange rinds are browned. Remove from heat and let cool. Add the orange rinds and slices of turkey bacon to a wooden skewer.

CETERA-STYLE
BLOODY MARY

Chef Cathy Wims of Nostrana in Portland, Oregon, shares her Italian twist on the classic. This recipe comes from the restaurant Il Convento in Cetara along the Amalfi Coast, a quaint little fishing village specializing in anchovy fishing. In southwestern Italy, Colatura, an Italian version of Asian fish sauce, is exemplary. Here, Chef Wims combines Colatura with the specialties of Amalfi—basil, tomato, and premium extra virgin olive oil, which are all enhanced by the vodka.

Serves 1

1½ ounces premium vodka (Monopolowa)
2 ounces San Marzano tomato juice
½ ounce fresh lemon juice
¼ ounce Colatura di Alici
cracked black pepper on top, and a light float of olive oil, basil leaf,
and a lemon wheel, for garnish

Chill a 12-ounce bucket or large rocks glass, then fill with ice.

In a cocktail shaker filled with ice, add the vodka, tomato juice, lemon juice, and Colatura di Alici. Lightly shake until just mixed. Strain the cocktail into the prepared glass. Garnish and serve.

JALAPEÑO BLOODY
—— MARY VERDE ——

Amishi Gadodia is a full-time food blogger from a small town in Indiana. Her site Naïve
Cook Cooks *is where she shares her passion for food, fashion, and traveling. She admits
she developed this savory and visually striking rendition of a Bloody Mary after getting
tired of being served bloodies containing super salty tomato juice from a bottle and cheap
vodka. Well, Amishi, we hope all those folks out there experiencing the same will pick up
this book and enjoy your delicious twist along with the many other recipes we feature.
Let's raise our glass to no longer settling for cheap, mass-produced Bloody Marys.*

Serves 1

Rim
lime wedge
Cilantro Salt, recipe on page 97

2 small to medium-sized tomatillos,
husked, washed clean, and chopped
1 small cucumber, peeled and chopped
½ Serrano chili pepper
3 or 4 sprigs fresh cilantro
½ teaspoon hot sauce

½ teaspoon Worcestershire sauce
(optional)
½ lime, juiced
1 pinch salt, to taste
1 pinch fresh ground black pepper,
to taste
1½ ounce Jalapeño-Infused Vodka,
recipe on page 97
celery stick, for garnish

In a blender, add the tomatillos, cucumber, chili pepper, cilantro, hot sauce,
Worcestershire, lime juice, and salt and pepper. Blend until smooth, and adjust
seasoning if needed.

Rim a Collins glass (page 13) with the Cilantro Salt, and fill the glass with ice. Add
the Jalapeño-Infused Vodka. Add the vegetable mixture from the blender and stir
well. Garnish and serve.

CILANTRO SALT

2 tablespoons fresh cilantro leaves,
  chopped
1 tablespoon salt

In a blender, add the cilantro and salt.
Blend until smooth.

JALAPEÑO-INFUSED VODKA

¼ cup premium vodka
1 jalapeño, seeded and sliced in half
  lengthwise

In a jar or sealed container with lid,
add the vodka and jalapeño. Refrigerate
for 2 or 3 days. Remove the pepper and
use as needed.

JAMAICAN ME CRAZY BLOODY MARY

General Manager Rob McShea of the Duck Dive Bar and Grill in San Diego, California, offers this tasty Caribbean-themed concoction every Tuesday evening. The inspiration comes from a recent trip to the farmers' market. Rob and his chef came across beautiful mangos and yellow heirloom tomatoes they couldn't resist. The marriage of these two ingredients reminded both of an experience at a Caribbean restaurant where jerk shrimp, mango chutney, and yellow tomato sofrito offered memorable flavor profiles. The takeaway here is that working with chefs expands your realm of recipe building as a bartender. Quality bartenders are able to balance cocktails and layer flavors, similar to a chef in the kitchen.

Serves 1

Rim
1 lemon wedge
jerk seasoning

1½ ounces Absolut Citron vodka
2½ ounces Yellow Heirloom Tomato Purée, recipe on opposite page
2 ounces Bloody Jerk Mix, recipe on opposite page
½ ounce agave nectar
2 jerk-rubbed prawns, mango chip, for garnish

Rim a Collins glass (page 13) with the lemon wedge and jerk seasoning, and fill with ice.

In a cocktail shaker filled with ice, add the vodka, Yellow Heirloom Tomato Purée, Bloody Jerk Mix, and agave nectar. Shake vigorously. Strain the Bloody Mary into the prepared glass. Garnish and serve.

YELLOW HEIRLOOM TOMATO PURÉE

2 large, ripe, yellow heirloom tomatoes, cored
1 teaspoon sea salt
1 teaspoon jerk seasoning

Purée the tomatoes using a blender or immersion blender until smooth, about 30 to 60 seconds. Season the purée with the salt and jerk seasoning. Blend again for 15 seconds to fold the seasoning into the purée.

BLOODY JERK MIX

1 ripe mango, skinned and pitted, cut into quarters
1 Scotch bonnet pepper
3 green onions, roughly chopped
1 ounce Worcestershire sauce
1 ounce quality fish sauce
1 ounce cider vinegar
1 teaspoon salt
1 teaspoon jerk spice

Start by grilling the mango flesh on a hot grill until both sides are caramelized. This will give the mango additional flavor when adding to the mix. Add the grilled mango into a blender along with the pepper, onions, Worcestershire sauce, fish sauce, vinegar, salt, and jerk spice. Purée until well blended, about 45 to 60 seconds.

— KEY WEST YELLOW MARY —

Executive Chef Daniel Higgins from the Hyatt in Key West, Florida, got together with his culinary team to create fun Bloody Marys for the annual Key West Food and Wine Festival. They jumped out of the box a little to experiment with colorful and flavorful mixes as well as different spirits other than traditional vodka. They ended up with three winning cocktails: Green Mary (featuring tomatillo, cucumber, celery, and tequila), the traditional Red Mary, with vodka, of course, and the Yellow Mary, made with rum, the official spirit of Key West. All three were a hit, but the stunning Yellow Mary stole the show.

Serves 5

6½ ounces fresh yellow tomato juice
1½ ounces yellow bell pepper juice
1½ ounces fresh pineapple juice (store bought is fine)
2½ ounces Yellow Beet Jus, recipe on page 102
1½ ounces fresh lemon juice
1 ounce mango nectar (store-bought is fine)
¼ ounce white balsamic vinegar
½ tablespoon prepared horseradish
1 or 2 dashes mango habañero hot sauce (available at large grocery stores)
½ teaspoon salt
¼ teaspoon white pepper
6¼ ounces white rum (Flor de Cana)
skewer of tropical fruit (pineapple, mango, etc.) and slices of golden beet, for garnish

Using a juicer, juice the tomatoes to extract the juice, and set aside. Follow the same procedure with the bell pepper and pineapple. In a large sealable container, add the tomato juice, bell pepper juice, and pineapple juice. Then add the Yellow Beet Jus, lemon juice, mango nectar, vinegar, horseradish, hot sauce, salt and pepper. Stir well to combine. Seal and chill in the refrigerator overnight. Strain through a chinois and stir in the rum. Pour over ice, garnish, and serve.

YELLOW BEET JUS

Makes about 5 cups

2½ pounds golden beets
salt, as needed
white pepper, as needed
2 cups fresh orange juice
2 cups sherry wine
1 cup white balsamic vinegar
1 ounce fresh tarragon, chopped
2 ounces fresh Italian (flat-leaf) parsley, chopped
1 ounce fresh chives, chopped
½ cup sugar

Preheat the oven to 400°F.

Rinse the beets under cold running water and drain. Toss the beets in a large bowl with salt and pepper to coat. Add the orange juice, sherry, vinegar, tarragon, parsley, chives, and sugar. Mix well and transfer the beets and liquid to a casserole dish or deep sheet pan. Roast in the oven until a toothpick can be inserted into the beets and easily removed, about 1 hour. Strain the liquid through a chinois and transfer to suitable container. Chill in refrigerator until ready to use. Use the beets for garnish or in a fresh garden salad.

—SRIRACHA BLOODY MARY—

If you enjoy Asian fusion and spice, this is the Bloody Mary for you. Sriracha, curry, ginger, wasabi powder, a dash of coconut milk—get ready for one tasty, zesty Asian-inspired cocktail. Blogger Kathy Bui of Builicious *grew up on traditional Vietnamese food so it's no surprise she reaches for Sriracha when she's looking for that extra kick. In fact, the iconic green-capped bottle of hot sauce never missed an appearance at the dinner table in her Vietnamese household. When she left home, she brought nothing with her but an air mattress, her favorite pair of jeans, and a bottle of Sriracha.*

Serves 4

8 pounds fresh ripened tomatoes (or 4 cups fresh tomato juice)
1 large ginger root, thinly sliced
1 cup Sriracha Hot Chili Sauce
1 cup sugar
½ cup coconut milk
1½ tablespoons curry powder
1 tablespoon salt
1 teaspoon wasabi powder
2 cups premium vodka
green onions, cucumber slices, lime wedges, for garnish

If using fresh tomatoes, cut the tomatoes in quarters and purée them in a blender or food processor until smooth. Strain and reserve the tomato juice.

In a large pot, combine the tomato juice, ginger slices, Sriracha, sugar, coconut milk, curry powder, salt, and wasabi powder. Simmer on medium heat for 10 minutes.

Remove the ginger slices and chill the mixture for at least one hour. Stir in the vodka, and pour into chilled pint glasses filled with ice. Garnish and serve.

—— KIMCHI BLOODY MARY ——

Different variations of Bloody Marys are Natalie Migliarini's obsession. She's a home bartender and professional party planner. Check her out online at BeautifulBooze. com. Natalie is always thinking outside the Bloody Mary box, so when she recently went shopping at her favorite Asian market and grabbed some kimchi off the shelf, she knew she had a new Bloody Mary in store. Kimchi adds ridiculous flavor to the drink and balances the tomato juice while the ginger adds a sweet and soothing quality. The seaweed garnish gives you a pre-drink snack that always makes for a notable cocktail experience.

Serves 2

½ cup kimchi
2 tablespoons rice wine vinegar
1 fresh lime, juiced
1 teaspoon fresh ginger, chopped
3 ounces premium vodka
10 ounces tomato or vegetable juice (V8)
½ teaspoon sesame oil
1 teaspoon Sriracha Hot Chili Sauce
Kimchi and toasted seaweed on a wooden skewer, for garnish

In a blender, add the kimchi, vinegar, lime juice, ginger, vodka, tomato (or vegetable) juice, sesame oil, and Sriracha. Blend well until smooth. Pour into two glasses filled with ice. Garnish and serve.

—LONG ISLAND BLOODY MARY—

In Montauk, New York, locals and visitors alike crowd the bar of Lynn's Hula Hut, a Polynesian-style tiki bar owned and operated by good friend Lynn Calvo. Her tiki journey began after traveling the globe and catering tiki-inspired events throughout the Hamptons and East End of Long Island from a sunset-orange truck outfitted with a thatched tiki bar. Today, her infusions and slice of island paradise are enjoyed by those looking for the best drinks around. One of those drinks happens to be her signature Long Island Bloody Mary, which is a delicious and refreshing twist on the iconic Long Island Iced Tea cocktail. If this concoction doesn't put a skip in your step, nothing will.

Serves 1

1 ounce Basil Syrup, recipe follows
½ ounce premium vodka
½ ounce premium tequila
½ ounce premium rum
¼ ounce premium gin
4 ounces Clamato juice (or try the homemade recipe on page 39)

2 ounces fresh lemon juice
1 pinch sea salt
1 pinch fresh ground black pepper
fresh basil sprig and lemon wheel, for garnish

Fill a large glass with ice. Add the Basil Syrup, vodka, tequila, rum, gin, Clamato, lemon juice, salt, and black pepper. Tumble into a cocktail shaker and then return to the glass, and use the rock and roll method—using two glasses, simply pour back and forth to give it a good mix. Garnish and serve.

BASIL SYRUP

1 fresh bunch basil leaves (about a palm full, rinsed and stems removed)
1 cup water

¼ cup agave nectar (or 1 cup brown sugar)

In a medium sauce pan over medium heat, add the water and agave nectar. Stir until the nectar is dissolved. Bring to a boil. Add the basil leaves and remove from heat. Let stand covered until the syrup is at room temperature. Strain the mixture (optional) into a suitable container and store in the refrigerator for up to 1 week.

MICHIGAN STATE'S BEST —— BLOODY MARY ——

In 2016, Abby Zamarripa of Latitudes & Steelhouse Sports Tavern in Howard City, Michigan, received the coveted Michigan's Best Bloody Mary Award. Abby grew up in a traditional Irish-Polish household where everything was made from scratch, from stewed tomatoes to home cooked/cured meats, which is the inspiration for this winning Bloody Mary. Latitudes Roadhouse and Steelheads Tavern is also famous for their Bloody Mary Bar, but the building is rumored to be haunted. Paranormal enthusiasts, including several ghost hunting television shows, have showed up over the years, seeking a ghostly encounter alongside their robust Bloody Mary cocktail.

Serves 1

Rim
Habañero Salt or Lime Salt

2 ounces premium vodka
8 ounces Michigan Bloody Mary Mix, recipe on page 108
Michigan Polish Roses (recipe on page 108), Michigan cheddar and Swiss cheese cubes, Michigan cherry tomatoes, sports peppers, chilled jumbo shrimp, Applewood smoked bacon, pickled asparagus, limes, pickles, green olives, for garnish

Rim a pint glass (page 13) with Habañero Salt or Lime Salt, and fill the glass with ice. Add the vodka and Michigan Bloody Mary Mix. Garnish and serve.

MICHIGAN BLOODY MARY MIX

46 ounces premium all-natural tomato
    juice
2½ teaspoons sea salt
2½ teaspoons fresh cracked black
    pepper
3 teaspoons Tabasco Hot Sauce
2 teaspoons Sriracha Hot Chili Sauce
1½ teaspoon A.1. Original Steak Sauce
2 teaspoons Worcestershire sauce
1 tablespoon dill pickle juice
2 tablespoons prepared horseradish
1½ teaspoons granulated garlic
½ teaspoon celery salt
½ fresh lime, juiced
½ fresh salad tomato, juiced

In a pitcher or suitable container,
add the tomato juice, sea salt, black
pepper, hot sauce, Sriracha, steak sauce,
Worcestershire sauce, pickle juice,
prepared horseradish, granulated garlic,
celery salt, lime juice, and fresh tomato
juice. Stir well to combine. Store in the
refrigerator until ready to use.

MICHIGAN POLISH ROSES

10 bundles wild ramps (or green
    onion)
1 (8-ounce) package soft cream cheese
1 package thin-sliced smoked ham

Clean the ramps thoroughly.
Spread a layer of cream cheese on 1
slice of ham. Roll up the ramp in the
ham/cream cheese slice, with white
part covered all the way and most
of the green part sticking out of the
bottom of the ham. (The ham is
the "rose" and the green stalk is the
"stem").

Continue with the rest of the ramps to
create a bouquet of "roses" if preparing
a Bloody Mary bar.

— MID-TOWN GREEN MARY —

When Billy Potvin and the Wayfarer American Grille in New York set out to develop their own twist on the Bloody Mary, they wanted to create a beautiful cocktail to complement their sophisticated setting and classic dishes, yet embrace the fun and frenetic energy of mid-town Manhattan. They succeeded. Today, this refreshing and healthy riff is served to patrons amid the bi-level restaurant, which boasts floor-to-ceiling windows overlooking the hustle and bustle of New York City.

Serves 1

Rim
chili powder
salt

2 ounces Cucumber-Infused Vodka, recipe on page 110
4 ounces Wayfarer Green Juice, recipe on page 110
red and yellow bell peppers and a celery stalk, for garnish

Rim a glass (page 13) with the chili powder and salt mixture, and fill the glass with crushed ice. Add the Cucumber-Infused Vodka and Wayfarer Green Juice. Garnish and serve.

CUCUMBER-INFUSED VODKA

Makes about 1 liter

English cucumber, peeled, seeded, and
    roughly chopped
1 (750-ml) bottle premium vodka

In a sealable container, like a 1-quart-
sized Mason jar, add the cucumbers
and vodka. Seal tightly and let sit 3 to
5 days, agitating the jar every other day.
Strain the vodka back into the original
bottle or another suitable container.
Store in the freezer.

WAYFARER GREEN JUICE

Makes juice for 3 to 4 servings

2 cucumbers
4 green apples, cored
16 kale leaves with stalks
1 lemon, peeled
2–3 pieces ginger

Using a juicer, juice the cucumbers,
apples, kale, lemon, and ginger.
Transfer to a sealed container and
store in the refrigerator. Shake before
serving.

MORNIN' MOONSHINE BLOODY MARY

While visiting Union Square Green Market in New York, Travis Brown, the former head bartender of Distilled NY, stumbled upon a cart filled with plump, vibrant, green and yellow heirloom tomatoes. This became the inspiration for his Mornin' Moonshine Bloody Mary. This cocktail is very pleasing to the eye because the color theme throughout is consistent while the garnish keeps the drink simple and the moonshine adds fun and freshness. Travis prefers using Ole Smoky Original Moonshine because the smoky flavor blends well with the ingredients.

Serves 1

MOON SPICE BLEND RIM

1 tablespoon sea salt
¼ tablespoon fresh ground black pepper
½ tablespoon sugar
1½ tablespoons ground Aleppo pepper

¾ ounce fresh lime juice
¾ ounce preserved lemon (page 162; you can also use lemon confit)
1½ ounces moonshine (Ole Smoky Original Moonshine)
Mornin' Moonshine Mix, recipe on page 113
speared pepperoncinis, for garnish

On a plate, combine the sea salt, black pepper, sugar, and Aleppo pepper. Rim a glass (page 13) with the Moon Spice Blend, and fill the glass with ice. Add the lime juice, preserved lemon, and moonshine. Top with the Mornin' Moonshine Mix, and mix well. Garnish and serve.

MORNIN' MOONSHINE MIX

6 tomatillos, husked and chopped
2 ripe yellow heirloom tomatoes
3 cloves garlic, peeled
1 dill pickle
3 dashes Green Tabasco Hot Sauce
¼ cup fresh cilantro leaves
1 Serrano chili, seeded
1 teaspoons sea salt
½ teaspoon sugar
1 tablespoon Aleppo pepper

In a blender, add the tomatillos, tomatoes, garlic, pickle, Tabasco, cilantro, Serrano chili, sea salt, sugar, and Aleppo pepper. Blend until puréed. Strain and refrigerate until ready to use.

——— NOLA VERDE MARY ———

There is nothing like a traditional brunch after fun a night out in New Orleans. When Melanie Glueck of the Red Fish Grill in New Orleans created the Nola Verde Bloody Mary, she envisioned a cocktail to accompany that typical Southern meal rich in Cajun flavor, butter, and spices. The following is a light and refreshing cocktail that leaves room for all the great food and fun that lie ahead.

Serves 5

7½ ounces Absolut Citron vodka
1½ cups tomatillos, peeled and chopped
2½ cups yellow heirloom tomatoes, chopped
1½ cups of yellow onion, chopped
2 garlic cloves, peeled
½ jalapeño, seeded
¼ bunch fresh cilantro leaves
1 tablespoon fresh lime juice
1 tablespoon coarse kosher salt
¾ tablespoons fresh ground black pepper
1 pinch celery salt
green onions, cilantro leaves, skewers featuring an assortment of olives, cocktail onions, pickled okra, cherry tomatoes, and cut jalapeños for a hat, for garnish

In a blender, add the vodka, tomatillos, tomatoes, onion, garlic, jalapeño, cilantro, lime juice, kosher salt, black pepper, and celery salt. Blend until smooth, about 3 minutes.

Fill five pint glasses with ice, then pour in the mixture. Garnish and serve.

PICO DE GALLO ——— BLOODY MARY ———

This Mexican-inspired Bloody Mary, crafted by Lynn Calvo of Lynn's Hula Hut in Montauk New York (page 106) is perfect for Cinco de Mayo. The fresh vegetable purée featured in this recipe is also terrific in ceviche or on a chilled steak salad.

Serves 4

8 ounces Cilantro, Cucumber, Jalapeño & Scallion Purée, recipe follows
6 ounces premium silver tequila (Don Julio)
2 ounce Cointreau
4 ounces fresh lime juice
16 ounces fresh heirloom tomato juice
1 pinch sea salt
lime wedge, for garnish

In a large pitcher, add the Cilantro, Cucumber, Jalapeño & Scallion Purée, tequila, Cointreau, lime juice, and heirloom tomato juice. Season with sea salt, to taste. Stir well to combine the flavors. Fill 4 pint glasses with ice, and add the mixed cocktail. Garnish and serve.

CILANTRO, CUCUMBER, JALAPEÑO & SCALLION PURÉE

1 cucumber, peeled and chopped
1 jalapeño, chopped
¼ cup fresh green scallions
½ cup fresh cilantro leaves
squeeze of fresh lime juice

In a NutriBullet or blender, add the cucumber, jalapeño, scallions, cilantro, and lime juice. Blend on high until the ingredients are puréed. Refrigerate up to 3 days.

Vincenzo Marianella and James O. Fraioli

ROASTED RED PEPPER MARY

Good friend and mixologist Jennifer Akin of the famed Alchemy Restaurant & Bar in Ashland, Oregon, who also shares her beloved Coconut Curry Mary (page 85), offers another twist using a medley of flavor combinations. In this savory concoction, Jennifer incorporates Roasted Red Pepper Purée, available at most markets or online, with organic chicken broth, which offers flavorful notes and incredible dimension to the drink. The kiss of garlic, kosher salt, and Homemade Rosemary Tincture finishes the cocktail with delicious umami and herbaceous flavors.

Serves 1

2 ounces premium vodka
2 ounces Roasted Red Pepper Purée
4 ounces Bare Bones Rosemary-Lemon Chicken Broth (or other organic chicken broth)
½ teaspoon garlic salt
½ teaspoon kosher salt

½ lemon, juiced
2 drops Homemade Rosemary Tincture, recipe follows
fresh rosemary sprig, red bell pepper spear, burrata cheese, and a pickled garlic scape, if available, for garnish

In a cocktail shaker or mixing glass filled with ice, add the vodka, Roasted Red Pepper Purée, Bare Bones Rosemary-Lemon Chicken Broth, garlic salt, kosher salt, lemon juice, and Homemade Rosemary Tincture. Stir well with a long-handled bar spoon until combined. Pour into a tall glass filled with ice. Garnish and serve.

HOMEMADE ROSEMARY TINCTURE

Makes about ¼ cup

¼ cup high proof vodka (or Everclear)
¼ cup fresh rosemary leaves

Add the rosemary to a suitable glass container or jar. Cover the rosemary with the vodka. Seal container and shake well. Store in a cool, dark place for 4 to 6 weeks, shaking the container periodically. Strain through coffee filters or cheesecloth into a clean dark glass container or jar. Store until ready to use. Note: The Tincture can be used after 8 hours, but will continue to gain potency if allowed to infuse for the maximum time.

— SHOTGUN BLOODY MARY —

Chef Erik Niel of Easy Bistro & Bar in Chattanooga, Tennessee, has a lot of respect for the Bloody Mary and its place in the world. Now that he's operating a bar and restaurant in the South, it's important to Chef Niel that his version of the iconic beverage includes a local favorite: Straight Rye Whisky. He also believes one should not neglect the tomato. Case in point: his signature Shotgun Bloody, which is driven by Chattanooga's sweet Sun Gold tomatoes. Chef Niel pickles them with champagne vinegar, rice wine vinegar, water, and sugar, and then cans them. He also preserves them with fresh thyme for the winter. The juice takes on the sweet tomato-ness of the Sun Golds, especially when blended with the Rye. Bulleit Straight Rye is the preferred choice because it has a great overall flavor that doesn't dominate the other ingredients while the spice of the rye is mild enough to augment the sweetness of the pickled Sun Golds.

Serves 1

1½ ounces Bulleit Straight Rye
1 ounce Sun Gold Tomato Purée, recipe on page 118
¾ ounce Sun Gold Pickled Juice, recipe on page 118
¾ ounce Worcestershire sauce
½ ounce fresh lime juice
1 pinch celery salt
1 pinch black pepper
3 or 4 dashes Cholula hot sauce
fresh Italian parsley, skewer of Pickled Sun-Gold Tomatoes (recipe on page 118) and a lime wedge, for garnish

In a glass filled with ice, add the rye, Sun Gold Tomato Purée, Sun Gold Pickled Juice, Worcestershire sauce, lime juice, celery salt, black pepper, and hot sauce. Stir well to mix. Garnish and serve.

SUN GOLD TOMATO PURÉE

4 cups Sun Gold cherry tomatoes, halved
8 small, crisp yellow tomatoes (Yellow Perfection) or 1 pound yellow pear tomatoes, halved or quartered (about 3 cups)
¾ teaspoon kosher salt

In a blender, add the tomatoes and salt. Blend until smooth and strain. Refrigerate until ready to use.

PICKLED SUN GOLD TOMATOES (WITH JUICE)

3 cups champagne vinegar
3 cups water
1 cup sugar
4 sprigs fresh thyme
1 sprig fresh lavender
2 cups fresh Sun Gold tomatoes, rinsed
salt and pepper, to taste

In a saucepot over medium-high heat, add the vinegar, water, sugar, thyme, lavender, and tomatoes. Season with salt and pepper. Bring to a boil. Remove from heat and transfer the hot contents to a Mason jar. Seal tightly, and let stand at room temperature for 2 to 3 hours to cool before storing in the refrigerator for up to 6 months.

SUNNY MARY

For those seeking a Bloody Mary on the lighter side, blogger and dinner party extraordinaire Barrett Bridenhagen of Dirty Laundry Kitchen says the trick is using fresh tomato water. Tomato water is delicate in flavor and body, which allows for a very elegant cocktail. Yes, making tomato water is admittedly more work than opening up a bottle of Bloody Mary mix, but don't give in to that temptation. Barrett's homemade tomato water from gorgeous yellow Roma tomatoes is the sumptuous ingredient that makes the Sunny Mary flavor so intense yet subtle. This drink also begs for fresh, raw garnishes rather than the heavy, pickled nibbles so make sure you go with what's in season. Barrett likes to add crisp cucumber sticks and cherry tomato halves.

Serves 4

---

2 cups fresh tomato water, recipe on page 121
1 lime, juiced
1 large dash celery bitters
¼ teaspoon celery salt
¼–1 teaspoon hot sauce (yellow mango habañero)
1 cup premium vodka
lime half wheels, cucumber sticks, cherry tomato halves, for garnish

Add the tomato water to a pitcher or suitable container. Add the lime juice, celery bitters, celery salt, and hot sauce. Stir well. Add the vodka, and taste. Add more or less vodka, depending on your preference. Stir well and pour into glasses filled with ice. Garnish and serve.

NOTE

Barrett uses a yellow mango habañero sauce for her hot sauce because she finds it to be the perfect taste and the right color. If you're too aggressive with a dark sauce, you could compromise the beautiful yellow color of the finished drink.

TOMATO WATER

Makes about 2 cups

1½ pounds fresh yellow Roma tomatoes
1½ teaspoons sea salt

Roughly chop the tomatoes, and add them to a colander set over a bowl or pitcher. Toss the tomatoes with sea salt. Let the tomatoes sit for several hours, stirring occasionally. When you have about 1½ cups of tomato water, and the tomatoes aren't dripping much when you stir them, remove the remaining tomatoes to a blender and purée. Strain ½ cup of the purée through a fine mesh into the tomato water. This will add a little more body while yielding about 2 cups of tomato water.

TURN UP THE BEET
—— BLOODY MARY ——

When Hangar 1 Vodka asked Coco Kelley *blogger Cassandra Lavalle to whip up a recipe for the perfect New Year's Day Bloody Mary, she rocked it. During the testing stage, she invited all the gals in her office to lend their opinion. The verdict? Delicious and gorgeous. Which secret ingredient makes Cassandra's drink so special? Beet juice, of course. In fact, the proportion of beet juice to tomato juice in this recipe makes the cocktail light, but not too earthy, and the bacon stick and salt rim, well, that's simply divine.*

Serves 2

Rim
lemon wedge
bacon salt
smoked paprika

4 ounces chilled Hangar 1 Straight Vodka (or other premium vodka)
Beet Bloody Mary Mix, as needed, recipe on page 124
hot sauce, to taste
pickled asparagus, kosher pickles, fresh rosemary sprig, celery, peppered bacon, small beets, pimento olives, pepperoncini, for garnish

Rim two glasses (page 13) with the bacon salt and a bit of smoked paprika, and fill the glass with ice.

In a cocktail shaker with minimal ice, add half the vodka (2 ounces), and top off with half the Beet Bloody Mary Mix. Add a dash or two, or more, of hot sauce, depending on your heat level. Shake and pour into the first prepared glass. Repeat the process for the second glass. Garnish and serve.

BEET BLOODY MARY MIX

Makes about 2 cups

1½ cups spicy tomato juice
½ cup pure beet juice
1 tablespoon pepperoncini juice (from jar)
½ lemon, juiced
1½ teaspoons fresh ground black pepper
½ teaspoon fresh horseradish, grated
1 teaspoon Worcestershire sauce
¼ teaspoon ground garlic

In a pitcher or suitable container, add the tomato juice, beet juice, pepperoncini juice, lemon juice, black pepper, horseradish, Worcestershire sauce, and garlic. Stir well to combine. Store in the refrigerator until ready to use.

"YELLOW IS THE NEW BLACK" —— BLOODY MARY ——

The Yellow is the New Black from New York's Upholstery Store: Food and Wine is one sumptuous cocktail created using only local ingredients from the world-famous Union Square Greenmarket where more than a hundred regional farmers sell their products to a dedicated legion of city dwellers. For the Upholstery Store, cocktail inspiration begins with what is fresh, intriguing, and unique. For the Yellow is the New Black, it starts with beautiful yellow tomatoes of the right consistency—not quite ripe. This offers a sweetness perfect for the Bloody Mary. Tequila is another vital component, which enhances the already floral and mineral-heavy palate experience of the yellow tomato. Without question, the color draws you in, the flavor piques your interest, and the Prosciutto Jerky's salty finish leads to a refill.

Serves 3–4

2 parts Basil-Infused Tequila, recipe follows

6 parts Bloody Mary Mixture, recipe on page 127

4 pieces Prosciutto Jerky, recipe on page 127

Thai basil, Prosciutto Jerky, mini mozzarella balls. Sprinkle top with a dash of crushed red pepper, for garnish

In a glass, add one large ice cube. Pour in the Basil-Infused Tequila and top with the Bloody Mary Mixture, allowing ½-inch or so of the ice cube to show on top. Stir, garnish and serve.

BASIL-INFUSED TEQUILA

Makes about 1 liter

1 (750-ml) bottle premium tequila (Tres Agaves Blanco)
1 cup basil leaves, tightly packed

Decant the tequila into a clean glass container with a tight-fitting lid. Rinse and dry the basil leaves. Add the leaves to the tequila. Keep the container away from the direct light and let infuse for up to 24 hours (at least overnight), or until the desired flavor is reached. Strain, remove basil leaves, and store in a glass bottle until ready to use.

BLOODY MARY MIXTURE

Makes about 1 quart

5 large yellow heirloom tomatoes, cut
    into eighths
2 fresh lemons, squeezed
1 tablespoon salt
1 tablespoon fresh black peppercorns
1 tablespoon cayenne pepper
1 tablespoon extra virgin olive oil
1 (1-inch) piece fresh horseradish,
    chopped
½ cup apple cider vinegar

In a blender, add the tomatoes, lemon
juice, salt, peppercorns, cayenne, olive
oil, and horseradish. Begin to purée,
and add the vinegar to help thin out
the mixture. Once smooth, pour
through a chinois strainer and use a
rubber spatula to extract all the liquid
until the mixture is dry and sticking to
the spatula. Store in a sealed container
in the refrigerator for up to 1 week.

PROSCIUTTO JERKY

prosciutto slices

Preheat the oven to 200°F.

Place the prosciutto slices between two
pieces of parchment paper and two
cooking sheets (to keep flat). Bake for
90 minutes, then pat dry of grease.
Remove from oven and let cool.

WATERMELON BLOODY MARY

You've got to hand it to Laurel Morley, food contributor to LaurenKelp.com, and the recipe and photography-driven blog Sweet Laurel, for coming up with this colorful and unique twist on the Bloody Mary. It's sweet, bright, and smooth with no canned tomato flavor or limp celery in sight. Laurel develops recipes out of her sunny kitchen in Phoenix, Arizona, where she began having daydreams about a beverage with the cool, sugary pink juice of a watermelon and the zesty kick of fresh lime juice, just a hint of salt, and the surprise spiciness of a fresh pepper. Then it hit her: if you add a splash of vodka and a garnish to this, it would create the perfect twist of the timeless classic.

Serves 2

2 cups watermelon cubes

¼ cup sugar

2 tablespoons fresh lime juice

1 jalapeño, stem removed (use a Serrano instead if you're feeling spicy)

3 ounces premium vodka

1 pinch salt

watermelon rind, grape tomato, jalapeño slice, fresh basil, for garnish

In a blender or food processor, purée the watermelon, sugar, lime juice, and jalapeño. Strain through a mesh strainer, reserving the juice.

In a cocktail shaker filled with ice, add the watermelon juice, vodka, and salt. Shake and pour into two glasses. Garnish and serve.

In this chapter . . .

OVER THE TOP

Some of us enjoy extravagant Bloody Marys, often loaded with entrées or so many garnishes they're more of a meal than a drink, and some of us don't. Whether you think the bartender went too far, or you're just unclear where the garnish ends and the buffet table begins, we've included just a sample of the many wonderfully outrageous Bloody Marys across America that you can drink—and eat. We begin with The Big Rib Bloody Mary from That Boy Good BBQ in Oceanside, California, which features a double-cut (two-bone) baby-back rib that pairs well with their house-made jalapeño-infused vodka. There's Milwaukee's Bloody Masterpiece, which boasts more than a dozen garnishes including a Polish sausage, Colby Jack cheese, chilled shrimp, and ground steak slider. The Sobelman's, who literally created the over-the-top Bloody Mary boom in the Midwest, truly impresses by defying gravity. We offer up Nantucket's Brant Point Grill's signature Bloody Mary with their horseradish-infused vodka and succulent meat from a two-pound lobster, as well as the Olympia Mary from American Charcuterie in Portland, Oregon, which is all about the pickle and pickled vegetables . . . and a pickled egg and cured meats. And finally, Sunda's Sumo Bloody Mary, Chicago's "Godzilla of Bloody Marys," is served in a 32-ounce Mason jar and tempts you with a smorgasbord of delectable garnishes including a grilled cheese sandwich, crispy pork belly, steamed bok choy, a sushi roll, spring roll, and much more. For those who appreciate "tailgates in a glass," enjoy these wild Bloody Mary creations!

——BIG RIB BLOODY MARY——

Chef Mark J. Millwood of That Boy Good BBQ in Oceanside, California, offers one filling cocktail thanks in part to his wife. Realizing their eatery served drinks to football fans coming in early to watch the games before the kitchen opened, Miss Kim had a brainstorm: make a Bloody Mary with food. The Big Rib features Mark's handcrafted Bloody Mary Mix with Miss Kim's suggestion of placing a double-cut (two-bone) baby-back rib over the top. Bon Appetit.

Serves 1

Rim
1 ounce TBG Rib Rub, recipe on
opposite page

Drink
2 ounces Jalapeño-Infused Vodka,
recipe on opposite page
1 ounce TBG BBQ Sauce, recipe on
opposite page
5 ounces TBG Bloody Mary Mix,
recipe on page 134

Garnish
Lime wedge on rim
1 celery stalk
2 pickled green beans
1 (6-inch) bamboo skewered with 1 olive
1 pickled Brussels sprout
1 double-cut (two-bone) BBQ
Smoked Pork Rib (recipe on page 134)
laid across the glass*

Rim a chilled pint glass (page 13) with the TBG Rib Rub, and fill the glass with ice.

In a cocktail shaker filled with ice, add the Jalapeño-Infused Vodka and TBG BBQ Sauce. Fill the remainder of the glass with TBG Bloody Mary Mix. Shake well and pour into the prepared glass. Garnish, add a straw, and serve on a small plate with a smile.

---

*Push the bamboo skewer through the middle of the ribs, securing them to the glass while presenting the olive and Brussels sprout on top.

TGB RIB RUB

1 pound brown sugar
1 cup white sugar
¼ cup smoked paprika
¼ cup onion salt
¼ cup garlic salt
¼ tablespoon cumin
1 tablespoon dry mustard
3 tablespoon coarse black pepper
2 tablespoons crushed red pepper

In a mixing bowl, add the brown sugar, white sugar, smoked paprika, onion salt, garlic salt, cumin, dry mustard, black and red pepper. Mix well to combine.

JALAPEÑO-INFUSED VODKA

5 fresh jalapeños, seeded and sliced
1 liter premium vodka

Add the jalapeños to the vodka. Seal and allow to steep for 2 days in a cool dark place. Remove the jalapeños early if you prefer less heat, or leave in longer for more heat.

TBG BBQ SAUCE

1 bottle Mexican Coca-Cola (made with real sugar not corn syrup)
1 cup yellow mustard
1 gallon ketchup
2 cups beef stock
½ cup Worcestershire sauce (Lea & Perrins)

1 cup cider vinegar
1 pound brown sugar
½ cup fresh lemon juice
1 cup molasses
1 cup roasted chili blend

In a heavy gauge saucepot, add the Coca-Cola, mustard, ketchup, beef stock, Worcestershire sauce, cider vinegar, brown sugar, lemon juice, molasses, and chili blend. Let simmer for 1 hour.

TBG BLOODY MARY MIX

½ gallon tomato juice (Campbell's)
¼ cup Worcestershire sauce
3 tablespoons prepared horseradish
     (liquid squeezed out)
1 tablespoon kosher salt
1 tablespoon coarse black pepper
1 lemon, zested and juiced
½ tablespoon Tabasco Hot Sauce
¼ cup olive brine (preferably from the
     green stuffed Spanish olives)

In a suitable container, add the tomato
juice, Worcestershire sauce, prepared
horseradish, kosher salt, black pepper,
lemon zest, lemon juice, hot sauce,
and olive brine. Mix well to combine.
Refrigerate until ready to use.

BBQ SMOKED PORK RIBS

1 rack baby back pork ribs
TGB Rib Rub
TBG BBQ Sauce

Chef Mark J. Millwood of That Boy
Good BBQ smokes his ribs at 225°F
for 3 hours. He first rubs the ribs with
a generous amount of the TBG Rib
Rub prior to going in the smoker. He
also uses an equal mix of hickory and
apple wood chips when cooking the
ribs, which are then basted with TBG
BBQ Sauce at the end.

— BLOODY MASTERPIECE —

Milwaukee is a city built on beer, and Dave and Melanie Sobelman's Sobelman's Pub & Grill is part of the historic landscape. Their famous street corner tavern is the original dispensary for what was once the bestselling beer in America, Schlitz, "The Beer that Made Milwaukee Famous." Aside from still selling plenty of beer, the Sobelmans are responsible for creating the Over-the-Top Bloody Mary boom in the Midwest. No surprise their pub is now a premiere destination for those seeking the ultimate Bloody Mary experience. Wanting to incorporate various foods from their neighboring vendors, particularly the Bay View Packing Company, the Sobelmans decided to build a Bloody with plenty of pickled garnish as a way to draw in bigger crowds while paying homage to their neighbors. One day, while loading up their skewers with pickled items, the Sobelmans realized they could take their beverage to a higher level by including one of their beef sliders. Today, on any given weekend, the Sobelmans will serve up five hundred Bloody Masterpieces. Clearly, as you'll see with this recipe, it's all about the garnish.

Serves 1

1½ ounces vodka (Titos)
8–10 ounces chilled Bloody Mary mix*

Garnish
Celery stalk
pickled Polish sausage
1-inch cube of Colby Jack cheese
cooked chilled shrimp
cherry tomato
lemon wedge

pickled Brussels sprout
pickled mushroom
pickled onion
pickled asparagus
pickle spear
green olive
green onion stalk
a fully cooked ground steak slider (with 2 slices of Colby Jack cheese, one each for the top and bottom bun so the slider stays together on the skewer)

Add the vodka to a 16-ounce ice-filled Mason jar and fill the remainder of the jar with Bloody Mary mix. Add the celery stalk to the jar. Using wooden kebab skewers and toothpicks, add the sausage, cheese cube, shrimp, tomato, and lemon wedge. On another skewer, add the Brussels sprout, mushroom, onion, asparagus, pickle spear, olive, and green onion, organizing like you would a floral arrangement. On a separate skewer, add the ground steak slider, and serve.

*Jimmy Luv's because its local, but you can also use one of the delicious handcrafted mixes in this book.

—LOBSTER BLOODY MARY—

Nantucket is synonymous with summertime on the East Coast, as the island fills up with souls seeking refuge from the city to soak up sun, fun, and clean salty air. Those who are craving fresh lobster and a good Bloody Mary don't need to look far, as the Brant Point Grill inside Nantucket's White Elephant Hotel offers both. You can have them together in one glass, too, as you'll see in this recipe.

Serves 4

Rim
smoked bacon salt

4 ounces Horseradish-Infused Vodka, recipe on page 138

4 ounces Pepper-Infused Vodka, recipe on page 138

1 quart Brant Point Signature Bloody Mary Mix, recipe on page 138

Garnish
Skewer of lobster meat (or small cracked lobster tails with meat), cherry tomatoes, and lemon wedges (see note below)

green olives

sprigs of fresh Italian parsley

lime wedges

dash of Togarashi seasoning mix

Rim 4 chilled glasses (page 13) with smoked bacon salt, and fill the glasses with ice. Pour 1 ounce of each of the vodkas into each glass. Top with Brant Point Signature Bloody Mary Mix, and stir. Garnish and serve.

NOTE ON LOBSTER GARNISH

Brant Point Grill uses one 2-pound live lobster. In a large pot, bring one gallon of salted water to a boil. Add the lobster and let simmer for 10 minutes. Remove the lobster and place in cold water to cool rapidly. Carefully remove the meat from the claws and tail using a lobster cracker to yield 1 pound of lobster meat. Then separate the meat into four portions and set aside. Cut a lemon into eight pieces and quarter about 20 cherry tomatoes. Place 2 ounces of lobster meat on each skewer, separating the meat with a cherry tomato, and top with a lemon wedge. Repeat for all skewers and put them in the refrigerator to chill before serving.

BRANT POINT SIGNATURE BLOODY MARY MIX

Makes about 1 gallon

1 gallon V8 Tomato Juice
2 ounces Worcestershire sauce
10 ounces fresh lemon juice
½ lemon, zested
¼ cup Sriracha Hot Chili Sauce
¼ cup prepared horseradish
2 ounces olive brine
½ teaspoon fresh ground black pepper
½ teaspoon celery salt

In a suitable container, add the V8 Tomato Juice, Worcestershire sauce, lemon juice, lemon zest, Sriracha Hot Chili Sauce, horseradish, olive brine, black pepper, and celery salt. Mix well to combine. Refrigerate until ready to use.

HORSERADISH-INFUSED VODKA

1 piece fresh horseradish, about 3 inches in length
1 liter premium vodka

Peel the horseradish and slice into 6 pieces. Add to a 1-quart Mason jar. Add the vodka, and tightly seal the jar. Store in a dark, cool place for 3 to 5 days, depending on the strength desired. Strain the vodka into a clean container and store until ready to use.

PEPPER-INFUSED VODKA

1 red jalapeño, seeded and sliced in half lengthwise (stem intact)
2 green jalapeños, seeded and sliced in half lengthwise (stem intact)
1 Serrano chili, seeded and sliced in half lengthwise (stem intact)
1 liter premium vodka

Add the peppers to 1-quart Mason jar. Add the vodka, and tightly seal the jar. Store in a dark, cool place for 5 to 7 days, depending on the strength desired. Strain the vodka into a clean container and store until ready to use.

OLYMPIA MARY

At Olympia Provisions—An American Charcuterie—in Portland, Oregon, they've mastered the pickle. They produce more than twenty different varieties of pickles throughout the year, based on seasonality and their Master Pickler's personal brine inspirations. Sometimes a hot jalapeño brine is used to kick things up while a sweet and spicy onion brine offers a savory punch. When Jessica Hereth introduced us to their Olympia Mary, we knew immediately a pickle brine would be included to offer the perfect balance of spicy, savory, and sour. The following recipe calls for a basic sour dill pickle brine. If you're not one who makes your own sour dills, McClure's Garlic Pickles provide an excellent brine for the Olympia Mary. You can also try a spicy giardiniera mix (available at most grocery stores), which provides a fun variety of pickles to add to the skewer. Better yet, join the Olympia Provision's Pickle of the Month Club for a year-long supply of pickle varieties and brines.

Serves 1

Rim
lemon juice
kosher sea salt
fresh ground black pepper

3 ounces tomato juice
2 ounces premium vodka
½ ounce pickle brine
1 teaspoon Worcestershire sauce
½ teaspoon prepared horseradish

¼ teaspoon fresh lemon juice
celery salt, to taste
fresh ground black pepper, to taste
1 or 2 dashes hot sauce (optional)

Garnish
1 skewer of pickled items such as pickles, zucchini, shallots, olives, cured meats (such as salami), and a pickled egg

Rim a pint glass (page 13) with the kosher sea salt and fresh ground pepper, and fill the glass with ice.

In a mixing glass, add the tomato juice, vodka, pickle brine, Worcestershire sauce, prepared horseradish, lemon juice, celery salt, black pepper, and the hot sauce, if desired. Stir well with a bar spoon and pour into the prepared glass. Garnish and serve.

Vincenzo Marianella and James O. Fraioli

—— SUMO BLOODY MARY ——

Considered the "Godzilla of Bloody Marys," the Sumo is the creation of Sunda's Executive Chef Jess DeGuzman. It's served in a 32-ounce Mason jar garnished with a massive cornucopia of Asian fusion meets Philippine street food. The Sumo is available only on weekends at Sunda, an award-winning restaurant in Chicago that serves up Eastern Asian and Southeast Asian fare. The key to crafting the Sumo Bloody Mary is to make sure to always stir, never shake.

Serves 1 (or more)

12 ounces fresh lime juice
2 ounces Sriracha Hot Chili Sauce
6½ tablespoons sugar
3 tablespoons salt
3 tablespoons fresh ground black pepper
3 ounces white vinegar
½ fresh cucumber
½ bunch fresh cilantro leaves
2 garlic cloves, peeled
½ fresh jalapeño, blended
4½ ounces Absolut Chicago (or Rosemary Infused Vodka, recipe follows)
1½ liters tomato juice

Garnish

grilled cheese (consisting of sweet pork, banana sauce, Japanese mayonnaise, and cheddar cheese)
crispy pork belly
bao bun (available in most Asian markets)
steamed rapini or bok choy
pickled Daikon (or American) radish
sushi roll (such as California or Broiled Crab Hand Roll)
small grilled green pepper (or Padron Chili)
a spring or egg roll

In a blender, add the lime juice, Sriracha, sugar, salt, black pepper, vinegar, cucumber, cilantro, garlic, and jalapeño. Blend on the lowest setting until well combined. Stir in (never shake) the tomato juice, add the vodka, and pour over ice in a 32-ounce Mason jar. Garnish and serve.

ROSEMARY-INFUSED VODKA

Makes 1 quart

1 quart premium vodka
5 fresh rosemary sprigs
3 green olives

In a quart-sized Mason jar (with lid and ring), add the vodka, rosemary, and olives. Seal with the lid and ring, and store in a cold dark place for 5 days.

THE VINCENZO COLLECTION

from Mixologist Vincenzo Marianella

As a renaissance barman and cocktail creator, I am all about fresh ingredients. I take the same pride making molecular cocktails as I do perfecting my juiced-before-your-eyes fruit and vegetable mixes—the secret component in my signature Bloody Marys. Trips to local farmers' markets are very important to me. Whether I'm after blood oranges, bushes of cilantro, or fresh pomegranate juice, farmers' markets provide me with fresh, delicious, organic produce along with plenty of cocktail inspiration. This has allowed me to dream up some amazing drinks while being a forerunner in the movement toward quality cocktails. The following Bloody Marys from my collection are perfectly balanced using nothing but fresh fruits, and vegetables. They are also very easy to make, and each is crafted using a particular spirit and Bloody Mary mix, which, of course, consists entirely of fresh herbs, fruits, and vegetables. I finish my Bloody Marys with simple, decorative garnishes—nothing over the top like the previous chapter—and depending on the specific Bloody Mary, I do like rimming the glass with a unique and colorful salt.

In this chapter . . .

CILANTRITA MARIA

Serves 1

Rim
Hawaiian black Vulcan salt

2 ounces premium tequila
½ ounce fresh lime juice
1 dash simple syrup
3 ounces Bloody Mary Mix, recipe follows
1 ounce organic green heirloom tomato juice
apple fan, small fresh cilantro sprig, for garnish

Rim a highball glass (page 13) with the Hawaiian black Vulcan salt, and fill the glass with ice. Add the tequila, lime juice, simple syrup, Bloody Mary Mix, and tomato juice. Stir well. Garnish and serve.

BLOODY MARY MIX

---

1 cucumber, peeled and chopped
2 leaves collard greens
1 green apple, cored and chopped
1 handful fresh cilantro

In a blender, add the cucumber, collard greens, apple, and cilantro. Blend until liquefied. Strain and store in the refrigerator until ready to use.

—— EVE'S GARDEN MARY ——

Serves 1

2 ounces premium vodka
½ ounce fresh lime juice
2 ounces coconut water
1 ounce Bloody Mary Mix, recipe follows
1 ounce organic green heirloom tomato juice
apple fan, 3 spinach leaves, very thin lime wheel, for garnish

In a highball glass filled with ice, add the vodka, lime juice, coconut water, Bloody Mary Mix, and tomato juice. Stir well. Garnish and serve.

BLOODY MARY MIX

2 apples, cored and chopped
2 cups spinach

In a blender, add the apples and spinach. Blend until liquefied. Strain and store in the refrigerator until ready to use.

—— GIN BLOSSOM MARY ——

Serves 1

Rim
Ginger Zing salt

2 ounces premium gin
½ ounce fresh lime juice
3 ounces Bloody Mary Mix, recipe follows
1 ounce organic red heirloom tomato juice
2 small cherry tomatoes, thin celery stick, with pomegranate seeds, ginger on the
stick, and slight dust of spirulina on top, for garnish

Rim a highball glass (page 13) with the Ginger Zing salt, and fill the glass with ice.
Add the gin, lime juice, Bloody Mary Mix, and tomato juice. Stir well. Garnish and
serve.

BLOODY MARY MIX

---

3 ounces organic pomegranate juice
1 ounce organic tart cherry juice
⅓ ounce ginger juice
½ spoon spirulina powder

In a suitable container, add the pomegranate juice, cherry juice, ginger juice, and
spirulina powder. Stir well until incorporated. Store in the refrigerator until ready to
use.

SWEET FANG MARY

Serves 1

Rim
Hawaiian green salt

2 ounces premium mezcal
½ ounce Grand Marnier
½ ounce fresh lemon juice
1 dash simple syrup
2 ounces Bloody Mary Mix, recipe follows
2 ounces organic Clamato juice (or make your own; page 39)
2 or 3 thin slices jalapeño, 1 spinach leaf, for garnish

Rim a highball glass (page 13) with the Hawaiian green salt, and fill the glass with ice. Add the mezcal, Grand Marnier, lemon juice, simple syrup, Bloody Mary Mix, and Clamato juice. Stir well. Garnish and serve.

BLOODY MARY MIX

1 handful fresh cilantro
½ jalapeño, seeded
2 cups spinach
1 apple, cored and chopped

In a blender, add the cilantro, jalapeño, spinach, and apple. Blend until liquefied. Strain and store in the refrigerator until ready to use.

— GLAMOUR GREEN MARY —

Serves 1

Rim
Persian blue salt (or kosher salt)

2 ounces premium gin
½ ounce St. Germaine
½ ounce fresh lemon juice
3 ounces Bloody Mary Mix, recipe follows
1 ounce organic green heirloom tomato juice
1 baby bok choy leaf, 2 grapes thinly sliced on top, for garnish

Rim a glass (page 13) with the Persian blue salt, and fill the glass with ice. Add the gin, St. Germain, lemon juice, Bloody Mary Mix, and tomato juice. Stir well. Garnish and serve.

BLOODY MARY MIX

½ broccoli crown, chopped
3 or 4 baby bok choy, chopped
4 ounces organic white grape juice

In a blender, add the broccoli, bok choy, and grape juice. Blend until liquefied. Strain and store in the refrigerator until ready to use.

—— LYCHEE LATINA MARIA ——

Serves 1

Rim
Danish smoked salt

2 ounces premium tequila
½ ounce lychee liqueur
½ ounce fresh lime juice
3 ounces Bloody Mary Mix, recipe follows
1 ounce organic yellow heirloom tomato juice
1 lychee, 1 basil leaf, 1 ¼-inch grapefruit slice, fennel seeds on top, for garnish

Rim a highball glass (page 13) with the Danish smoked salt, and fill the glass with ice. Add the tequila, lychee liqueur, lime juice, Bloody Mary Mix, and tomato juice. Stir well. Garnish and serve.

BLOODY MARY MIX

4 or 5 basil leaves
1 fennel bulb
6 ounces fresh organic grapefruit juice

In a blender, add the basil, fennel, and grapefruit juice. Blend until liquefied. Strain and store in the refrigerator until ready to use.

— MINTY MARIANNE MARY —

Serves 1
---

2 ounces premium gin
½ ounce fresh lime juice
1 dash simple syrup
3 ounces Bloody Mary Mix, recipe follows
1 ounce organic green heirloom tomato juice
basil and mint sprig, 2 thinly sliced cucumber wheels, thin slice ginger, for garnish

In a highball glass filled with ice, add the gin, lime juice, simple syrup, Bloody Mary Mix, and tomato juice. Stir well. Garnish and serve.

BLOODY MARY MIX

1 large cucumber, peeled and chopped
5 or 6 fresh basil leaves
15–20 fresh mint leaves
1 (1-inch) piece ginger, peeled

In a blender, add the cucumber, basil, mint, and ginger. Blend until liquefied. Strain and store in the refrigerator until ready to use.

—— QUENCH ME MARY ——

Serves 1

Rim
rock salt (optional)

2 ounces grapefruit vodka
½ ounce fresh lemon juice
3 ounce Bloody Mary Mix, recipe follows
1 ounce organic orange heirloom tomato juice
thin bell pepper, kale leaf, thin carrot strip laid on top or wrapped around inside of
glass, for garnish

Rim a glass (page 13) with the rock salt, and fill the glass with ice. Add the grapefruit
vodka, lemon juice, Bloody Mary Mix, and tomato juice. Stir well. Garnish and
serve.

BLOODY MARY MIX
---

3 or 4 kale leaves
3 or 4 carrots, peeled and chopped
1 small red bell pepper, chopped

In a blender, add the kale, carrots, and red bell pepper. Blend until liquefied. Strain
and store in the refrigerator until ready to use.

—— VELVET KRAKEN MARY ——

Serves 1

Rim
roasted garlic salt (optional)

2 ounces basil vodka
½ ounce fresh lime juice
3 ounces Bloody Mary Mix, recipe follows
½ ounce organic Clamato juice (or make your own; page 39)
⅓ ounce squid ink, more or less to taste
grilled-charred small octopus tentacle, 3 or 4 arugula leaves, for garnish

Rim a glass (page 13) with the roasted garlic salt, and fill glass with ice. Add the basil vodka, lime juice, Bloody Mary Mix, and Clamato juice. Stir well. Garnish and serve.

BLOODY MARY MIX

1 small beet, chopped
2 cups arugula
1 apple, cored and chopped

In a blender, add the beet, arugula, and apple. Blend until liquefied. Strain and store in the refrigerator until ready to use.

WISE MARY ───

Serves 1

Rim
Peruvian blue salt

1 ounce Pear William liquor
1 ounce cucumber vodka
½ ounce fresh lemon juice
3 ounces Bloody Mary Mix, recipe follows
1 ounce organic green heirloom tomato juice
apple and pear fan (3 slices each), 2 thin cucumber wheels, mustard seeds, for garnish

Rim a highball glass (page 13) with the Peruvian blue salt, and fill the glass with ice. Add the Pear William liquor, vodka, lemon juice, Bloody Mary Mix, and tomato juice. Stir well. Garnish and serve.

BLOODY MARY MIX

2 green apples, cored and chopped
1 mustard green leaf
2 celery stalks, chopped
1 small handful fresh cilantro

In a blender, add the apples, mustard green, celery, and cilantro. Blend until liquefied. Strain and store in the refrigerator until ready to use.

MICHELADAS & SHOOTERS

Many of you have probably heard about or tasted the michelada, a refreshing Mexican beverage made with beer, fresh lime juice, and assorted sauces, spices, and peppers, often served in a chilled, salt-rimmed glass. With micheladas, basically a spinoff of the traditional Bloody Mary, fresh-squeezed citrus is critical while tomato juice is optional. In this chapter, we feature the Cozy Cove, arguably one of the top thirst-quenching summertime cocktails out there, best made with Modelo beer. Empellon Al Pastor in New York serves a collection of signature micheladas, including the featured recipe with Victoria beer and a passion fruit-habañero mix. Timna's Moroccan Michelada, also showcased, is about spice, topped off with a Stigel Goldbrau lager. When it comes to shooters, the basic concept is to pack as much flavor as you can inside a small, compact vessel like a shot glass. The Cove Bar and Grille in South Carolina prefers filling their shot glasses with fresh select oysters, premium and infused tequila, and house-made mixes. Food blogger Cheyanne Bany also prefers using fresh seafood, as you'll find in her Spicy Bloody Mary Gazpacho & Shrimp Shooters, while food blogger Daniel George adds a little Shiraz wine to his unique Bloody Mary–style shooter.

In this chapter . . .

— COZY COVE MICHELADA —

There are many variations to this delicious cocktail throughout Mexico and Latin America, some of which contain tomato juice. This particular recipe comes from good friend and cocktail aficionado Roger Ebner, who has proven to us that you can't drink just one of these, so make sure you have enough beer and limes on hand.

Serves 1

Rim
lime wedge
seasoned salt (Lawry's)

1 fresh lime, juiced
1 or 2 dashes seasoned salt (Lawry's)
2 or 3 dashes Tajin Clásico Seasoning
1 or 2 dashes Worcestershire sauce
1 beer (Modelo)
lime wedge or wheel, for garnish

Rim a chilled glass (page 13) with the seasoned salt, and fill the glass with ice. Add the lime juice, seasoned salt, Tajin, and Worcestershire sauce. Slowly pour in the beer. Mix with a bar spoon until blended and frothy. Garnish and serve.

—— WINEY MARY SHOOTER ——

Daniel George, the man behind the food blog MANtitlement, is a cocktail guy who appreciates a good Bloody Mary and loathes red wine. He's also the one at the party who never really sits down, always in the kitchen whipping up some sort of concoction for his guests. And for parties, he likes to make shots. Because Shiraz is always in the house— it's his wife Christie's go-to red wine so there's plenty to go around—Daniel attempted to combine her drink with his and turned it into a shot. The result is the Winey Mary Shooter. Surprisingly, the Shiraz elevates the flavor profile of the tomato juice. Now Daniel can finally say he enjoys red wine—so long as it's mixed into a Bloody Mary.

Makes 4 (2-ounce) shots

Rim
Jalapeño Salt, recipe follows

3 ounces high-quality Shiraz
2 ounces premium vodka
3 ounces tomato juice

1 teaspoon Worcestershire sauce
1 teaspoon fresh lemon juice
½–1 teaspoon Sriracha Hot Chili Sauce
(depending on your heat preference)
1 pinch salt
1 pinch fresh ground black pepper

Rim each shot glass (page 13) with the Jalapeño Salt.

In a cocktail shaker filled with ice, add the Shiraz, vodka, tomato juice, Worcestershire sauce, lemon juice, Sriracha, salt, and black pepper. Shake well and strain into the prepared shot glasses.

JALAPEÑO SALT RIM

8 teaspoons kosher salt
1½ teaspoons onion powder
1½ teaspoons garlic powder

1 pinch celery seed
1 pinch cumin
½ cup powdered jalapeño pepper

Pour the salt into a blender or food processor and process for a minute and a half, or until fine. Add the onion powder, garlic powder, celery seed, cumin, and jalapeño powder. Pulse until well mixed.

EL CUÑADO "BROTHER-IN-LAW" MICHELADA

Noah Small of Empellon Al Pastor in New York enjoys exploring flavor combinations that combine well with beer and present themselves in the "michelada" tradition. In this interesting spin on the michelada, named after "that guy you have to take around because he's your brother-in-law," the combination of passion fruit and habañero chilies is Yucatecan in its inspiration. Noah prefers to remove the seeds from the chilies and then cook the flesh to bring out the real flavors of the habañero. Despite its famous heat, when the seeds are removed, floral notes emerge. It's great in combination with the passion fruit. Noah also opts to use Victoria for the beer component, but any lighter lager will do. Pacifico, Mexicali, and Modelo Especial all work well if Victoria is not available.

Serves 1

1½ ounces Passion Fruit-Habañero Mix, recipe follows
Victoria Beer (or other Mexican lager)

Fill a chilled beer or pilsner-style glass with ice. Slowly add the Passion Fruit-Habañero Mix, and top with beer.

PASSION FRUIT-HABAÑERO MIX

canola or vegetable oil, as needed, for deep frying

1 or 2 habañero chilies*
1 cup passion fruit purée

Slice open the chilies and remove the seeds. In a small saucepot over high heat, add enough canola or vegetable oil to deep-fry the chilies. When the oil is hot, carefully add the chilies and deep-fry until soft, about 1 minute. Remove the chilies from the oil and drain on paper towels, making sure to eliminate any remaining oil on the flesh of the chilies. Add the chilies to a kitchen blender along with the passion fruit purée. Blend until the chilies are incorporated, about 1 to 2 minutes. Transfer to a sealed container and store in the refrigerator for up to 1 week.

* It's important to wear gloves when working with habañeros (or any hot chili pepper).

—— MOROCCAN MICHELADA ——

To craft a michelada that truly reflects the heritage of Timna's chef/partner Nir Mesika, who grew up in Israel, but whose family's roots are Moroccan, Amir Nathan incorporates traditional Moroccan ingredients such as preserved lemons and Chef Nir's house-made harissa, a fiery North African hot chili paste. At the New York restaurant, the Moroccan Michelada is built in a mixing glass with the harissa, preserved lemon, and lemon juice, and shaken well before being poured into a pint glass and topped with Stigel Goldbrau lager. To entice the diners' palates for upcoming dishes, Amir rims the glass with smoked paprika and salt. Recently, Timna's modern approach to Israeli and Moroccan fusion earned the restaurant Winner of USA Today's *Best New Restaurant in America "Readers' Choice" Award.*

Serves 1

Rim
1½ teaspoons smoked paprika
1½ teaspoons kosher salt

2 teaspoons Smoked Harissa, recipe on page 162
1 tablespoon Preserved Lemon, recipe on page 162
¾ ounce fresh lemon juice
1 light lager or pilsner (Stigel Goldbrau)
Lemon wheel, for garnish

Rim a chilled pint glass (page 13) with the smoked paprika and kosher salt, a.k.a. Smoked Paprika Salt. In a separate mixing glass, add the Smoked Harissa, Preserved Lemon, and lemon juice. Shake vigorously. Pour into the prepared glass, and top with beer. Garnish and serve.

SMOKED HARISSA

4 red bell peppers
6 garlic cloves, peeled
1 teaspoon smoked paprika
1 teaspoon cumin
1 teaspoon soy sauce
1 teaspoon Worcestershire sauce
1 cup canola oil
3 tablespoons white vinegar
3 dashes Tabasco Hot Sauce
kosher salt, to taste
fresh ground black pepper, to taste

Place the peppers over an open flame and grill until all of the skins are burned and blistered. Remove from the flame and let cool. Remove the seeds and place in a blender. Add the garlic, smoked paprika, cumin, soy sauce, and Worcestershire sauce. Blend until well puréed. Transfer the mixture into a large pot over very low heat. Add the oil, and let simmer for 3 hours, stirring occasionally, about every 20 minutes. Add the hot sauce and season with salt and black pepper. Remove from heat and store in a sealed container in the refrigerator for up to 3 weeks.

PRESERVED LEMON

5 lemons
4 tablespoons kosher salt
1 teaspoon cilantro seeds
2 bay leaves

Wash the lemons well, and thinly slice. Place a single layer of lemon slices in the bottom of a clean jar or suitable container with lid. Cover the slices with some of the salt, cilantro, and bay leaves. Add another layer of lemons and repeat the process until all the lemon slices are used up. Seal the jar or container, leave outside for 3 days, then place in refrigerator for 3 weeks. When the lemon skins are soft, they are ready to use.

OYSTER SHOOTERS
— (CALIENTE OYSTER & BAJA OYSTER) —

At The Cove Bar and Grille in North Charleston, South Carolina, they are all about oysters. Chef Keith Haynes leads a Cajun-inspired menu that embraces the region's bountiful oysters and the influences he brought with him from New Orleans. One of their more popular items, especially during weekends, is the Caliente Oyster Shooter, made with House-Made Jalapeño-Infused Tequila and House-Made Bloody Mary Mix. This shooter is a twist on their traditional and very popular Baja Oyster Shooter. Both recipes are included and both shooters are perfect for crowds because you can make them in advance and in large quantities.

BAJA OYSTER SHOOTER

Serves 1

1 small select oyster
1 shot premium silver tequila
House-Made Margarita Mix, as
    needed, recipe on page 164
lime wedge, for garnish

In a kosher salt–rimmed double shot glass, add the small oyster. Add the tequila and float the mix on top. Garnish and serve.

CALIENTE OYSTER SHOOTER

Serves 1

1 small select oyster
1 shot House-Made Jalapeño-Infused
    Tequila, recipe on page 164
House-Made Bloody Mary Mix, as
    needed, recipe on page 164
lemon wedge, for garnish

In a salt-rimmed double shot glass, add the small oyster. Add the tequila and float the mix on top. Garnish and serve.

HOUSE-MADE MARGARITA MIX

Makes about ¾ cup

½ cup sour mix
¼ cup triple sec
¼ tablespoon fresh orange juice
¼ tablespoon lemon-lime soda
4 lime wedges, juiced

In a small container, add the sour mix, triple sec, orange juice, lemon-lime soda, and the lime juice. Mix well to combine and store in the refrigerator in a sealed container until ready to use.

HOUSE-MADE JALAPEÑO-INFUSED TEQUILA

Makes about 1 liter

3 medium-sized jalapeños
1 (750-ml) bottle premium silver
    tequila

Thinly slice the jalapeños, making sure not to discard the seeds. Add them to a 1-quart Mason jar. Seal the lid tightly and shake vigorously. Store in a dark place for 2 to 3 days, and up to 1 week for maximum heat. Pour tequila through a mesh strainer to remove the jalapeños and seeds. Transfer to a clean container, seal, and store for up to 3 weeks.

HOUSE-MADE BLOODY MARY MIX

Makes about 1 pitcher

2 quarts tomato juice
½ cup cocktail sauce
3 tablespoons horseradish
4 lemons, juiced
4 limes, juiced
2 tablespoons fresh ground pepper
1 tablespoon celery salt
1 tablespoon seasoned salt
1 tablespoon Worcestershire sauce
¼ cups jalapeño juice

In a pitcher, add the tomato juice, cocktail sauce, horseradish, lemon juice, lime juice, pepper, celery salt, seasoned salt, Worcestershire, and jalapeño juice. Mix well to combine and refrigerate until ready to use.

SPICY BLOODY MARY GAZPACHO & SHRIMP SHOOTERS

These visually stunning shooters are complements of blogger Cheyanne Bany of No Spoon Necessary. *They combine her love of sharing a meal with family, which always involves Bloody Marys, with her affinity for fresh seafood. These shooters taste fantastic while offering nibbles in a cocktail, which makes them a little dangerous because it's easy to forget they contain alcohol. These savory sips are like a tiny private party for your sights and taste buds.*

Serves 20

Rim
lime wedge
fresh ground black pepper (optional)

Spicy Bloody Mary Gazpacho, recipe on page 167
Spicy Bloody Mary Roasted Shrimp (recipe on page 168), fresh dill sprigs,
lemon or lime wedges, cucumber sticks or wedges, jalapeño
pepper sticks or rings, for garnish

Rim the shot glasses (page 13) with the black pepper. Pour the gazpacho into a measuring cup, or any container with a spout, to cleanly transfer gazpacho into the glasses. Garnish and serve chilled.

SPICY BLOODY MARY GAZPACHO

Makes about 4½ cups

½ roasted red bell pepper, roughly chopped
½ cucumber, peeled and roughly chopped
1 stalk of celery, with leaves, roughly chopped
¼ red onion, peeled and diced
1 pound ripe cherry tomatoes (gold and red), halved
1 clove garlic, peeled and minced
½ teaspoon salt
¼ teaspoon fresh ground black pepper
½ teaspoon sugar
¾ teaspoon celery salt
1 teaspoon Worcestershire sauce
1 tablespoon fresh lime juice
1 tablespoon extra virgin olive oil
1 tablespoon prepared horseradish
½–1 teaspoon Tabasco Hot Sauce, according to taste (or use 1 seeded and
diced jalapeño)
1½ cups Bloody Mary mix (Zing-Zang Bloody Mary Mix, or try one of the mix
recipes in this book)
2–3 ounces premium vodka
salt and pepper, to taste

In the bowl of a food processor, fitted with a steel blade attachment, pulse the red
bell pepper until coarsely chopped. Be careful not to overprocess. Transfer to a large
mixing bowl. Repeat the process for the cucumber, celery, onion, and tomatoes. Add
to the bowl the garlic, salt, black pepper, sugar, celery salt, Worcestershire sauce, lime
juice, olive oil, horseradish, hot sauce, Bloody Mary mix, and vodka. Stir thoroughly
to combine. Transfer half the mixture back to the bowl of the food processor. Purée
until smooth, about 1 to 2 minutes. Add the puréed gazpacho back to mixing bowl.
Mix and adjust seasoning, according to taste, with salt and pepper. Cover with
plastic wrap and refrigerate for at least 2 (up to 6) hours to allow flavors to marry.
Taste for seasoning again before serving.

SPICY BLOODY MARY ROASTED SHRIMP

1 cup Bloody Mary mix (Zing-Zang Bloody Mary Mix, or try one of the
mix recipes in this book)
2 teaspoons Worcestershire sauce
½ teaspoon Tabasco Hot Sauce
½ teaspoon celery salt
½ teaspoon garlic powder
½ teaspoon fresh ground black pepper
20 fresh wild-caught large shrimp, peeled, deveined and tail left intact

In a medium-sized mixing bowl, or large ziptop bag, add the Bloody Mary mix, Worcestershire sauce, hot sauce, celery salt, garlic powder, and black pepper. Add the shrimp, and let marinate in the refrigerator for 30 minutes to 1 hour, stirring half way through the marinade time.

Preheat oven to 425°F.

Prepare a sheet pan by lining it with aluminum foil for easy clean up. Drain shrimp and discard marinade. Place shrimp, in a single layer, on the sheet pan. Roast shrimp until pink in color and cooked through, about 5 to 8 minutes. Be careful not to overcook.

ABOUT THE AUTHORS

VINCENZO MARIANELLA is an Italian renaissance barman and one of the most celebrated mixologists in America. After playing professional basketball in Italy, Vincenzo worked at bars in Australia, New York, and London before permanently relocating to Los Angeles in 2005. Before Vincenzo, the cocktail scene in LA, compared with New York and London, was a sticky wasteland of sweet-and-sour mix, triple sec and bottled lime juice. Then Vincenzo stepped behind the bar at Providence, started using fresh herbs, fruits, and vegetables, and changed everything. He opened Copa d'Oro in Santa Monica and in 2006 launched his cocktail consulting business MyMixology with partner Zahra Bates. Vincenzo, who believes he's not in the bar industry, but the hospitality industry, is best known for his versatility in cocktails, from a simple gin and tonic to molecular mixology.

JAMES O. FRAIOLI is an award-winning cocktail and cookbook author with twenty-five cookbooks to his name, including the 2014 James Beard Award winner *Culinary Birds*. His titles have been featured on the Food Network and *The Ellen DeGeneres Show*, and have appeared on dozens of national radio shows, including Martha Stewart Living Radio. They have received further praise from publications such as *Forbes Travel Guide, Reader's Digest, Oprah Magazine,* and the *New York Times*. Prior to his career as a culinary book author, James served as a contributing writer and editor for dozens of food and wine publications, and has more than 250 feature articles to his credit. Visit him online at www.culinarybookcreations.com.

INDEX

176

CONVERSION CHARTS

METRIC AND IMPERIAL CONVERSIONS

(These conversions are rounded for convenience)

Ingredient	Cups/Tablespoons/ Teaspoons	Ounces	Grams/Milliliters
Butter	1 cup/ 16 tablespoons/ 2 sticks	8 ounces	230 grams
Cheese, shredded	1 cup	4 ounces	110 grams
Cream cheese	1 tablespoon	0.5 ounce	14.5 grams
Cornstarch	1 tablespoon	0.3 ounce	8 grams
Flour, all-purpose	1 cup/1 tablespoon	4.5 ounces/0.3 ounce	125 grams/8 grams
Flour, whole wheat	1 cup	4 ounces	120 grams
Fruit, dried	1 cup	4 ounces	120 grams
Fruits or veggies, chopped	1 cup	5 to 7 ounces	145 to 200 grams
Fruits or veggies, puréed	1 cup	8.5 ounces	245 grams
Honey, maple syrup, or corn syrup	1 tablespoon	.75 ounce	20 grams
Liquids: cream, milk, water, or juice	1 cup	8 fluid ounces	240 milliliters
Oats	1 cup	5.5 ounces	150 grams
Salt	1 teaspoon	0.2 ounces	6 grams
Spices: cinnamon, cloves, ginger, or nutmeg (ground)	1 teaspoon	0.2 ounce	5 milliliters
Sugar, brown, firmly packed	1 cup	7 ounces	200 grams
Sugar, white	1 cup/1 tablespoon	7 ounces/0.5 ounce	200 grams/12.5 grams
Vanilla extract	1 teaspoon	0.2 ounce	4 grams